Love's Braided Dance

Love's Braided Dance

Hope in a Time of Crisis

NORMAN WIRZBA

Yale UNIVERSITY PRESS

New Haven and London

Published with assistance from the foundation established in memory of Henry Weldon Barnes of the Class of 1882, Yale College.

Yale University Press books may be purchased in quantity for educational, business, or promotional use. For information, please e-mail sales.press@yale.edu (U.S. office) or sales@yaleup.co.uk (U.K. office).

Set in Minion type by Integrated Publishing Solutions.
Printed in the United States of America.

Library of Congress Control Number: 2024932059
ISBN 978-0-300-27265-9 (hardcover : alk. paper)

A catalogue record for this book is available from the British Library.

This paper meets the requirements of ANSI/NISO Z39.48-1992 (Permanence of Paper).

10 9 8 7 6 5 4 3 2 1

For Lila

Contents

Love's Braided Dance

Introduction

The Way of Hope

Whoever is joined with all the living has hope.

—Ecclesiastes 9:4

It was supposed to be a short holiday, the last boating excursion of the season for Carmine and Rosaria Menna to join with six of their closest friends to enjoy the pleasures of the sea. Their plan was to remain in sight of the coast of Lampedusa, their small island home in the Mediterranean, located between Italy and Tunisia. A luxurious evening swim in a cove, along with the gentle rocking of the boat, had provided a good night's rest. The dawn promised a sunny and peaceful day in which to cruise about and fish. But when Carmine emerged on deck, his peace was interrupted by the squawking sound of what he thought to be a flock of seagulls. When his friends joined him on deck, they said, "Something is screaming."[1]

It wasn't seagulls they heard. It was people, hundreds of them, thrashing in the water, yelling with all their might, desperate for help. As Carmine steered his boat to the scene, he and his companions encountered the floating debris of a sunken vessel, along with discarded clothing and shoes. They saw the dead. They saw faces gasping and choking; many of those struggling were clearly exhausted. How long had they been in the water? The sea writhed from so many people kicking and flailing to stay afloat. How long before they lost the energy to keep trying? Carmine thought to himself, "They are all drowning. I can't possibly save them all." His boat, the *Galata,* was built for a maximum of ten people. Neither Carmine nor his friends had any training in ocean rescue. They also knew there are strict laws against aiding illegal immigrants.

Carmine and his friends eventually managed to pull forty-six men and one woman on board (they later learned that many of the migrant women and children had been trapped below deck, and drowned when their boat went down). So many hands begged to be grasped. So many agonizing choices had to be made. The friends decided to focus their efforts on clusters of people rather than on individuals, knowing that their decisions to rescue some consigned others to death. There wasn't much time. Those still alive had swallowed a lot of seawater and were visibly sick and exhausted. Their bodies were covered with a film of diesel fuel, making them slippery to hold on to. As more migrants were pulled on board, their weight risked capsizing the *Galata.*

Like many others living in the Mediterranean region, Carmine knew that thousands of migrants tried to reach European shores every week. He also knew that many of them died in the attempt. The Mediterranean is known to be the world's deadliest border, claiming over 30,000 migrants' lives since the year 2000, with many more victims unaccounted for. When Carmine heard news reports about the migrant crisis, he often turned the radio off. He wanted to live his own life, take care of his family, and keep his focus on his optometry business. Carmine didn't speak badly of the migrants that came upon Lampedusa's shores or, like some others, complain publicly about how their presence was destroying local tourism. But he didn't visit them at the town reception center either. He was shy and reserved, not the sort of person who hugged freely.

Carmine was surprised by the visceral attachment he suddenly felt pulling the first young man aboard. He wanted to hug and comfort him, like a protective parent. To this day, he has not forgotten the feel of the young man's hand in his, nor the power that flowed through his body as he reached out to grab hold of yet another person, wanting and willing each of them to survive. He says he never felt more alive in his life than at that very moment. His muscles tingled and his nerves sparked with energy. When the coastguard finally came, he could not fathom the captain's order to stop the rescue effort. Nothing in him wanted to steer the *Galata* back to shore.

Months later, Carmine said, "I can still feel the fingers of that first hand I seized. How they cemented into mine, bone grinding against bone, how they clamped down with such a grip that I saw the sinuous veins of the wrist pounding. The force of that hold! My hand in a stranger's hand, in a bond stronger and more intimate than an umbilical cord. And my whole body shaking with the force of the hold as I pulled upwards and dragged the naked torso from the waves." It was the touch of another's hand and the feel of another's flesh that activated within him the power he describes as love. When the *Galata* came to shore and the migrants were taken by police and emergency staff to the reception center, he wanted to stay with them. "He wanted to take their hands again, to talk to them. He wanted to sit down with them, to ask how they were, who they were, why they'd come. He wanted to know if the fishing boats or the coastguard had found their families, if they'd been reunited with their loved ones. He had to know what happened. He would not give up on them."[2]

In the days and weeks that followed, Carmine and his friends were overcome by grief. Each suffered in one way or another, with nightmares, panic attacks, insomnia, anger, or depression. Carmine had never felt such emotional intensity or sorrow. He also knew more pain was still to come because more boats would be coming every day, more hands grasping for help. Reporters came knocking, wanting to "get the story," but Carmine wasn't interested in being portrayed as a hero. Replaying in his mind over and over again that terrible time, seeing the floating bodies of the dead (a total of 368 people died that day), and later learning that other boats ignored their cries for help, Carmine feels that he failed these people. Indeed, the cultures of Europe were failing these people. It wasn't lost on him that these migrants came from Eritrea, a former colony of Italy.

The scene of rescue was also a scene of disaster because it signaled decades of Western economic and imperialist policies that weakened the local institutions of former colonies, decimated traditions, displaced landholders, created millions of refugees—and then made them feel unwelcome when they fled hunger and fear and hopelessness. The rapid and recent creation of border walls in Europe—in 1989 there were fifteen fortified walls, but by 2016 there were almost seventy, with several more being planned—and the growing violence being directed at migrants indicated a startling failure to recognize and welcome these migrants as human beings, a striking refusal to offer help to others in need.[3] As Carmine reflected on the day of rescue, he finally came to see these migrants as people who had a claim on his life. He insists that he was no one's savior. Instead, Carmine discovered how deaf he had been to the cries for help that sounded in his world, and how willfully ignorant he was about the policies and pressures pushing people to make the heart-wrenching, family-fragmenting choice to flee their homes.

In an important sense, the migrants he rescued also rescued him because they put him in touch with life's meaning and purpose. They helped him recognize that the priorities by which he had organized his life needed to change. What he now knew was that he had an active role to play in creating a more hospitable world, a world that welcomed strangers and offered help to those who needed it. The migrants were strangers, but he came to feel a bond with them that went beyond friendship. "The people he had rescued were on the brink of existence. And when he held their hands in his, when he watched them take their first breaths on the *Galata*'s deck, he knew he had touched the very essence of life. They had looked him in the eye and they had chosen to live."[4]

The survivors didn't stay in Lampedusa. They were eventually moved on to destinations farther north. Carmine worried for them because he knew that a warm welcome was unlikely wherever they went. He knew that the refugee camps and detention centers they would meet along the way would chip away at their dignity and self-respect. Would the countries and communities that allowed them to stay also embrace them and partner with them in the construction of a new life?

A year later, several came back to be with Carmine and his friends. They wanted to visit the site of the tragedy. The reunion was tearful and joyous. One survivor came running to Rosaria, embraced her in a tight hug, and showed her the T-shirt she had given him when he was first pulled on to the *Galata*. It was the token of kindness he kept and needed as he journeyed through the degradations of refugee camps and detention centers. Two others presented a piece of paper to the group. "It was a simple but beautifully executed drawing of a grasping hand coming out of the water and being met above by another hand which clasped it in a fierce grip."[5]

The friends and survivors sailed on the *Galata* to visit the site where they had first been brought together. When they arrived at the scene, the survivors asked that everyone join hands. Some prayed. Some sang. Some threw flowers into the ocean. Some sobbed. As they prepared to return to shore, one of the teenagers pointed to the water and said that was where he died. He pointed to the deck of the *Galata* and said that was where he was reborn.

According to the United Nations High Commissioner for Refugees (UNHCR), roughly one in 74 people were displaced in the year 2022 (compared to one in 159 in 2010), reaching the unprecedented total of 108.4 million people displaced worldwide. These are people who had to flee their homes because of war, persecution, economic injustice and collapse, and a changing climate. Of this number, 62.5 million people were internally displaced, meaning they remained within their country of origin and had some hope of returning to their homes.[6]

Many others, however, cannot hope to return home. They live in stalled, uncertain, and often dangerous situations, neither able to return home nor able to move to a suitable destination elsewhere. As the Canadian-American journalist Matthieu Aikins has observed, "Those who are forced abroad usually don't get far. More than four-fifths of the world's refugees are hosted in the developing world, where borders and humanitarian aid from wealthy countries keep them in place. From this dammed-up pool of the displaced, the West takes measured sips."[7]

A simple number puts these "sips" in perspective: in 2022 only 114,300 people (out of the roughly 45,900,000 refugees, asylum-seekers, and those needing international protection) were resettled in third countries. The rest were confined to camps and detention centers where squalor, disease, hunger, boredom, anger, violence, and anxiety often run rampant, places named by the journalist and filmmaker Bernard-Henri Lévy as the *anus mundi* of our time.[8] They have little choice, since they know that the "smugglers' road" is extremely dangerous, with smugglers often extorting, raping, and abandoning clients. They know that the borders blocking their escape are heavily guarded and violently enforced. Patrick Chamoiseau describes these borders as being "sharpened more and more like the blade of a guillotine."[9]

I recognize that the current percentage of people worldwide attaining this level of displacement and desperation is relatively small. But relative to what measure? How many is an "acceptable" number of refugees, especially when we dispense with statistical thinking and keep our focus on the personal losses and tragedies of each refugee's life? How should we think about the economic and political policies that are destroying homes and long-practiced ways of life and thereby creating a growing refugee population? What should be said to the political and business elites that are fully committed to the free movement of capital but fully opposed to the free movement of people? These questions are becoming more and more urgent each year because demographers now project that, owing to climate change and the social unrest and political conflict it will unleash, roughly 1.2 billion people worldwide will be displaced by the year 2050, roughly one out of every eight people on earth.[10]

To think that displacement and desperation are problems only for those officially deemed "migrants" or "refugees" would be a mistake. People can feel displaced or adrift even while inhabiting what looks to be a home if they are not receiving the care and support they need. Maybe they feel that they don't belong or that their lives don't matter. They can be in a gathering of people and know that no one notices them or would miss them if they were to disappear. They can be citizens and sense that governments and business leaders do not care about the health of their bodies, the future of their grandchildren, the condition of their neighborhoods, or the safety of their food or water. They can become desperate when they feel abandoned and despised or when they sense that a commendable future is open to others but closed to themselves. They can lose hope when they feel they are trapped in cycles of abuse and systems of injustice.

As these examples show, desperation and displacement are not simply descriptors that can be applied to some people in extreme circumstances. They can also refer to an everyday condition that determines the feel of life itself, a sense of being abandoned, abused, and alone. When people ask for help and do not receive it—think here of the 368 Eritreans desperately reaching for a rescuing hand—hope is denied. When people are too afraid or lack the energy to raise their hands at all, hope dies.[11] This is why so much depends, as Carmine came to understand, on whether people can learn to turn to others, genuinely face them, commit to working for their good, and extend a welcoming hand.

Hope is an inherently vulnerable way of being. People need to know that they and their communities are valued and cared for. Where care is not forthcoming or, more drastically, where people feel invisible or abandoned, hope is hard to sustain. For it to grow and strengthen, people need to feel the loving touch of another. For hope to be more than an abstract idea or possibility, people need to see love going to work where they are.[12] They also need the help of each other to interpret what is happening, since people, especially in contexts of emotional and moral turmoil, often lack the ability to discern the truth of their own lives.

The quiet and often unremarked desperation that many ordinary people feel is on a continuum with the desperation that Carmine encountered off the coast of Lampedusa because they each represent a form of abandonment. We could even argue that the latter is the near-inevitable logical fulfillment of the former, which is why it is so important that we bring into view, and then address, the practical conditions that are producing so much human sadness and loneliness. Put another way, refugees give us a window into the wider and systemic cultural malfunction that produces the suffering that, to varying degrees, affects millions more. Refugees are "canaries in the coal mine" telling us to create cultures of welcome and nurture lest we destroy ourselves and our world. Today's global refugee crises are not somehow aberrant or exceptional. We must avoid thinking of them that way.

From a historical point of view, the extended helping hand has often been an ambiguous and morally fraught gesture. What may have appeared, and even been meant, as a hospitable gesture has sometimes turned into a fist that subjugates and violates those it touches, or a grip that stifles and restricts their development. Think here of the missionaries that came to save "lost" Indigenous peoples but ended up destroying their communities. Think also of the international financial and development agencies that came with the promise of a better future but ended up erasing the traditions and institutions that gave people a meaningful and praiseworthy life. As these examples show, good intentions are not enough. A better way is when people approach each other and their shared worlds in the gentle postures of humility and solicitude, postures not based on a presumption that any of us knows beforehand or definitively what others need. Solicitude requires that people be willing to be with others, to listen to them, to be instructed by them, and then to discover together with them what needs to be done so that mutual flourishing might be achieved.

As I understand it, the name for this way of being is love. Love is the hope-producing power that guides our minds, hearts, and hands when it is activated in us. With love, hope is not only kindled but catches fire. Love fires up hope because love refuses to abandon others or leave them to die. Recall the young Eritrean man who knew he would die if a hand did not reach out to him and pull him back into life. The deck of the *Galata* was the site of his rebirth because that is where he felt the love that affirmed his life as worth saving and supporting. Recall also that Carmine was pulled back into life by the power of the love that was activated in him when another hand grasped hold of his. The clasping of two hands, and the feel of the power of life circulating through that shared embrace, created an awakening within him: he now realized how precious life is and how worthy it is of being cherished.

Hope has no future apart from a skilled and practiced cherishing of life. The life that needs cherishing, however, isn't only each and every human life. Our vision and our sympathies need to expand to include the many plant, insect, and animal species we share our life with because human life depends upon, and only makes sense in terms of, every life. We cannot truly love our neighbors if we do not also love the neighborhoods—the houses and community centers, the gardens and parks, the fields and forests, the foodsheds and watersheds—that make our life together possible. In other words, our most fundamental, abiding, and pressing task is to build multiple versions of the *Galata*, multiple sites all around the world for the restoration, reconciliation, and redemption of living beings.

The future of hope, I believe, depends on the activation of love, love that is inspired by the grace of this life, love that is committed to the cherishing of our shared places. Love requires that we work to overturn programs of displacement and patterns of violation that leave people abandoned and abused. Love requires that we reject the economies that render people desperate and alone and instead develop the capacities—above all, the sympathies and affections—that will inspire people to create communities of mutual flourishing. As the biblical sage Qoheleth put it, hope resides in our joining with all the living. This joining would be a loving embrace of each other and our shared places. It would be what the Kentucky poet and farmer Wendell Berry describes as a plighted life, a life in which people, by pledging themselves to care for each other, become braided together.

> The way I go is
> marriage to this place,
> grace beyond chance,
> love's braided dance
> covering the world.[13]

A logic governs the way of hope. It is difficult to articulate because the way of hope is not linear, systematic, or smooth. It does not follow twelve neatly defined steps that, when taken in succession, lead a person into a hopeful manner of being. Instead, it is often meandering and circuitous as people attempt to live faithfully and mercifully with each other. False starts, improper motivations, and harmful choices, but also felicitous decisions, serendipitous encounters, and enduring commitments, often reveal themselves only along the way. This is why this book's chapters take the form of essays that explore paths into what I take to be hope's animating logic. My aim is to narrate the experiences and journeys of various people so that the heart of a hopeful way of being can come into view.

These chapters, then, are complementary sketches that together draw a picture of what a hopeful life looks like, or, more exactly, they offer a series of improvisational movements that make a compelling theatrical performance in which hope appears. As people go through life, what do they encounter, what should they accept, how should they respond, and to what end? Hope registers as the desire to celebrate and further the loveliness and love-worthiness of this life. When we live a hopeful life, love animates what we do and why we do it.

The way of hope is inspired by an acknowledgment of what can be called the miracle or grace of life itself, the realization that your own life and the lives of others are the never-again-to-be-repeated embodied expressions of life's primordial, gifted goodness. Affirmation of the love-worthiness of this world is the spark that ignites a hopeful way of being because it calls people to give their love to the world in return. When love is given, the prospect, but not the guarantee, of a better future emerges. Imagine how the lives of displaced and desperate people would be transformed if family members, neighbors, teachers, co-workers, shopkeepers, politicians, and law-enforcement officials treated them with courtesy and respect and did everything they could to create the built environments (the homes, parks, farms, schools, health-care facilities, workplaces) to help them explore and realize their unique potential. Imagine how displaced people would feel if those they encountered took the time to know them deeply and thereby communicated that they were worthy of being loved.

Hope does not rest on the assumption that everything is going to work out or be all right in the end, nor is it based on the presumption that the outcome in any series of events is going to be thus and so. I agree with Berry, who says, "Hope lives in the means, not the ends."[14] A hopeful life often moves in the dark because nobody has a clear grasp of how events will unfold or what effects any particular action will have. This is why hope is a humble posture. It moves in what can be called the optative mood—"if only . . . "— expressing a desire for a better world, a world in which the relationships joining people to each other are governed by attention and affection.

To say that hope is humble is not to say that it is weak. Authentic hope takes courage and perseverance as people commit to changing the contexts that generate despair. The philosopher Jonathan Lear has called this kind of hope "radical hope" because it signals a commitment to work for a world that often exceeds anyone's current ability to understand it, and a resolve to work for a future that in many of its details remains unknown.[15] This form of hope requires a creative imagination to picture what currently seems like an impossible future, and it requires a committed heart that does not easily give up when obstacles to the realization of this future emerge. When hope takes this radical form, grief and lament are not forms of resignation in the face of this world's pain and violation. They are, instead, forms of power that fuel a person's commitment to "join with all the living" and offer a healing hand of help.

Hope and optimism are not the same thing. In fact, optimism often works against hope because it does not sufficiently acknowledge or protest against the injustices that currently degrade and destroy life. As the literary and cultural critic Terry Eagleton has persuasively argued, optimists tend to be rather conservative in their outlook and all too accepting of the status quo. They put their trust in the "essential soundness of the present" and do not have the creativity or energy to work for a more praiseworthy future.[16] There can be a fundamental blindness, even dishonesty, in the cheery optimist's outlook because it does not properly name or adequately account for the injustices of the past or the present.

Hope is a way of being in which people commit themselves to the healing of our wounded world and, in so doing, communicate a future that is worth striving for. It is an orientation and a disposition that is animated by the power of love that affirms the sanctity of this life and this world. It does not forsake or abandon this world with the evasive, escapist fantasy of some other world. This would be a false hope founded on a fundamental disdain for the life we have been given. Instead, hope grows as love becomes a quotidian, economic force that spreads across the world.

Hope germinates wherever and whenever love goes to work. It grows as love takes root in each person's world and in each person's life. It flowers and fruits when people feel the power of love nurturing and healing the communities in which they live.

1
Erotic Hope

Admonitions to "Be hopeful" can, like a soporific, lull people into accepting the status quo. Suitably pacified, hopeful individuals simply wait for the miracle that will in some hypothetical, perpetually deferred future make everything all right. The Indigenous philosopher Kyle Whyte instructs us to be cautious around these (often comfortable and satisfied) purveyors of hope. Their calls to hopefulness can generate what he calls the "ultimate bystander effect," by giving people an excuse not to do the hard work of correcting the injustices that create hopelessness in the first place.[1]

Think, for instance, of the generations of religious leaders who have told their followers to accept suffering and endure every hardship because God will, in the end, make everything right. Pains will eventually be healed and injustices corrected, provided that people are patient and put their hope in God. Think, too, of the business tycoons and technology gurus who tell their followers that a technological fix will always, inevitably, get people (at least those who can afford it) out of whatever troubles they find themselves in.

My point is not to deny God or trash technology. It is to indicate that people have not been well served by these expressions of "faith" that keep them passive or reduced to being little more than spectators of their own lives, mostly deaf to the world's cries for healing and help, and thus exempt from the work of creating a more hopeful future.

Assurances of hope can be seductive. I regularly sense their power when I am in conversation with people about some of the most weighty and challenging issues of our time, issues like anthropogenic climate change, environmental degradation, species extinctions, ongoing racism, sexism, and income inequality, pandemics, the tearing of social fabrics, political polarization, and the widely reported increases in personal stress, anxiety, depression, and despair. It is not hard to become paralyzed by sorrow and fear when faced with these many forms of eco-socio-system collapse. This may be why such conversations eventually make their way to the question "What gives you hope?" A compelling answer will, presumably, help us all feel better.

I am no longer sure that "What gives you hope?" is the right question to be asking. The problem with this question is that it can make hope seem like a thing we can pick up along life's way. Some people have it. Some people don't. The key is to find it, hold on to it tightly, and (ideally) pass it along to those who are without it. The temptation, then, is to think that hope works like a shield or, less combatively, a security blanket that protects people from the many troubles of this world. I understand the temptation. I, too, want assurances that everything, somehow, no matter what, is going to be all right. My concern with this framing, however, is that it casts hope as something that people acquire, like a vaccine that renders people immune to this world's suffering.

But what if hope isn't really, or at least not fundamentally, a thing to possess? What if hope is, instead, a loving way of being that is animated by an affirmation of the goodness of this life, a practiced way of life rooted in the conviction that this life is worth cherishing, defending, and celebrating? How does our thinking and living change when hope is characterized more as a verb and less as a noun?

Let's shift the question, then, from "What gives you hope?" to "What do you love?" and "How does this love change what you hope for?" I make the shift because conversation and reading have taught me that people who live in hope do not seek to shield themselves from the pains and problems of this life. Their love compels them to engage the trouble and work for a better future. Hope grows, and its meaning is more fully discovered, when love goes to work in the world. The most important matter is not that people have a fully worked-out picture of what a better world looks like or have a clear sense of the exact form their action should take. The most important thing is to act on the conviction that your community needs you and is calling you to contribute in some way. To ask people what they hope for also has the merit of opening a space for two further important questions that bear directly on living a hopeful life: "What inspires or activates your hope?" and "What are the practical conditions that optimize a hopeful way of being?" It is hard to see how hope has a future unless we have someone to love and places to cherish and unless we feel the love of others. Hope becomes inauthentic the moment it ceases to be moved by love.

The stories of the people who inspire hope in others often follow a similar narrative arc. Think, for instance, of the Swedish environmental activist Greta Thunberg, who describes how at age eight she first heard about climate change and what it meant for the life of this planet. It put her into a deep depression. She stopped talking. She didn't eat. She couldn't understand why politicians, educators, and business leaders were not doing everything they could to address what, in her mind, was the most important crisis humanity has ever faced. One day, years later, she followed the advice she now regularly gives to others: "Act. Do something!" On August 20, 2018, she went to the Swedish parliament buildings, sat down with a sign, and initiated the first "school strike for climate." Before she knew it, and in ways that she still does not fully understand, her action went viral on social media. Others sat down with her. Journalists came to interview her. School strikes began in other Swedish cities and then in other countries. Two months later, tens of thousands of students from around the world were joining her by striking and marching down their city streets. A little over one year later, an estimated four million students and adults in 170 countries participated in a Global Climate Strike.

The American congresswoman Alexandria Ocasio-Cortez shares a similar story. Having finished college, she worked at multiple jobs, all the while becoming more and more depressed about the structural inequalities and injustices she encountered. She recalls wallowing in despair, wondering if her life would amount to anything more than showing up, doing some work, going home, and then doing it again and again. The tipping point came when she went to Standing Rock, North Dakota, to protest the construction of a gas pipeline. There, simply by standing with hundreds of ordinary people all committed to stopping this violation of an Indigenous community's ancestral lands, Ocasio-Cortez says she felt a newfound power that was liberating. "From there I learned that hope is not something that you have. Hope is something that you create, with your actions. Hope is something that you have to manifest into the world, and once one person has hope, it can be contagious. Other people start acting in a way that has more hope." Thunberg agrees, which is why she says direct action "is the best medicine against sadness and depression."[2]

Thunberg and Ocasio-Cortez, along with many others, teach us that hope and action are inseparable and that they are held together by a yearning for a different world. There are no guarantees that the world hopeful people desire will come about or that the world they desire is the best one, which is why hopeful action is an inherently risky endeavor that is subject to frustration, disappointment, and correction, since our loves are often malformed or misdirected, or a species of wish-fulfillment. The crucial thing, as Rebecca Solnit has argued in her insightful book *Hope in the Dark,* is that people not think hope is like a lottery ticket. Hope is a power that propels people off the couch and out the door. "Hope calls for action; action is impossible without hope . . . To hope is to give yourself to the future, and that commitment to the future makes the present inhabitable."[3] Stories of hope are fundamentally love stories, she says, which is why it is so important not to lose sight of love. "It's the well that you drink from, the touchstone that reminds you who you are and why you're here."[4] Hope is born in spaces of vulnerability as people open themselves to, and allow themselves to be moved by, whatever trouble and whatever goodness are happening around them. It grows as they give themselves to sharing life's beauty with others and as they learn how best to care for each other while in the midst of the trouble.

If you ask, "What can you give to the future?" people might wonder if they have much that is worth giving or if whatever giving they do really matters. They might worry that what they have to give will not be well received. In an essay, "Uses of the Erotic," Audre Lorde observes that oppressive contexts stifle a desire to love deeply and commit wholeheartedly. They do this by distancing people from the wells of feeling that are deep within, stifling their sympathy and care for others, and smothering their joy and delight in others and in themselves. Women in particular have been told to distrust and suppress these feelings as worthless, irrational, and dangerous. When people distrust and suppress feelings, life becomes a matter of going through the motions. Whatever people do and accomplish lacks passionate commitment and deep satisfaction. By becoming (or being made) numb to themselves and their world, people slowly lose the sense that who they are and what they do really matter. Life, says Lorde, becomes stripped of its erotic power and value, and people lose the desire to engage deeply and get involved.[5]

Erotic love has nothing to do with a pornographic culture. In fact, the pornographic impulse can be described as the enemy of genuine eroticism because it objectifies and degrades others, rather than honors and celebrates them. Pornography represents a preference for mere sensation over sympathetic feeling. The erotic, by contrast, refers to the life force and the creative energy that propel people to risk giving themselves to others. Sometimes it takes the form of the body and soul rapture people feel when they first encounter a beloved other. Sometimes it is the feeling of being so immersed in and consumed by a creative activity—preparing a meal, writing a poem, playing a game, exploring an idea, planting a garden—that time vanishes. Eroticism is not about the ability to exercise power over others but about the ability to engage and share the various powers of life with others. It is about being caught up within flows of life we find to be beautiful and good. This is why Thunberg and Ocasio-Cortez both spoke of how important it was to them, and how inspiring and sustaining it was, to know that they were not alone in the struggle, that they had companions to encourage them along the way, and that they were involved in something bigger than themselves.

The outcome of true eroticism is shared joy, a delight in and celebration of life's freshness, vitality, resilience, goodness, and beauty. People experience joy when they feel themselves most fully alive, actively participating in the life all around, and exercising the potential that is uniquely theirs to realize. When joy is real and deep, it frees bodies to explore and dance.

It manifests itself, for instance, in the exuberance of a child being amazed by a tiny frog along a creek bed, or in the deep satisfaction a teacher feels helping students make the discoveries that will set them off on their vocational paths. It becomes real in the profound pleasure and contentment a person can feel knowing they are beloved by others, or in the intense ache a person feels being in the presence of a beautiful flower that is already starting to wilt. The opposite of joy isn't sadness. It is numbness and the erosion of the yearning for intimacy.

To experience joy people must be willing to open and give themselves to life's surprising and sometimes unsettling possibilities. For many people this prospect is fearful because it places on them a demand that they live in such a way that their feelings are affirmed and that their endeavors are, as Lorde says, "in accordance with that joy we know ourselves to be capable of." When people become attuned to the feelings of sympathy and care that can be activated within them, they have a lens through which to examine all aspects of their existence. Are we living to the fullest, working to realize the potential that is latent within ourselves and others? Lorde recognizes that "this is a grave responsibility, projected from within each of us, not to settle for the convenient, the shoddy, the conventionally expected, nor the merely safe." But when erotic power goes to work, "it flows through and colors my life with a kind of energy that heightens and sensitizes and strengthens all my experience."[6]

For erotic power to have the chance of going to work, however, people need the support of a loving community that affirms and encourages them. Beginning in childhood, but continuing throughout their lifespan, they need nurturing spaces in which they can explore and fail and know that they will not be ridiculed and abandoned. Individuals are much better prepared to take risks and give themselves to their communities when they know that others will accompany them along the way.

One of the most profound articulations I know of the relationship between love, hope, and community can be found in the apostle Paul's letter to his congregation in Corinth. Throughout the letter Paul expresses his concern that people are not living together in a harmonious and mutually empowering manner. Instead, they are divided and fighting with each other, with some claiming superior status. The result? People are alienated from each other, and joy is absent. Paul believes that the division and rancor that characterize this congregation communicate a basic confusion about what it means to live well. It isn't simply that they are mistaken about this or that issue—for example, what and how to eat, how to navigate grievances, and what genuine leadership is—but that they have failed to understand what it takes to live an authentic, fulfilling, and hopeful human life.

Paul assumes that people cannot flourish alone because the nature of reality is inherently communal. Life and loneliness, he would say, are incompatible with each other. People may find themselves existing alone, but isolated or fragmented existence is hardly the ideal context in which a deep feeling for life's beauty and vitality can grow. Life's mysteries and splendors, what we might also call its ever-fresh potential, are discovered as people work to be genuinely with each other and, in this work, nurture and strengthen the bonds that join them.

Paul's position is hard to appreciate, especially after we have been shaped by decades of neoliberal teaching about individual freedoms and choices as the essentials of life. As epitomized in the widely influential writings of Ayn Rand, "winners" in life are self-motivated, self-sufficient, self-legislating, and self-legitimizing beings. The heroes described in her novels are ardent individualists who deny that anyone besides themselves has a rightful claim upon their time or energy. Their goal is to have the courage to live for themselves and not be dependent on anyone else. Rand believed that if a person achieved success, it was because of that person's initiative and prowess. The flipside, of course, is that if a person failed, it was entirely their own fault.

This neoliberal framing of life isn't simply an idea. It has taken root in economic and political policies that have undermined institutions dedicated to providing opportunities for communal help and thriving. Community groups still exist, but participation in them is entirely voluntary. People may join for a while, but there is little expectation that anyone will stay for the long term, especially if individual preferences change or the community becomes disagreeable in some way. Neoliberal assumptions have become so pervasive that church leaders now recognize that their attendees are regularly in a "church shopping" mode. It doesn't take much for someone to leave.

Paul describes a genuinely human life in a radically different manner. To make the point he gives his followers a powerful image: everyone is to be so intimately joined to everyone else, and so committed to each other's well-being, that together they make and move as one organic living body. He tells his followers that "you are the body of Christ and individually members of it" (1 Corinthians 12:27). In a healthy body there are many diverse members, but the diversity does not prevent the body from moving as a harmonious whole so long as the love of Jesus inspires and animates them. Diversity is the body's strength and vitality, enabling it to manifest a wide variety of gifts and talents. In Christ's body, every part matters, even the parts that may seem insignificant. (We know this simply by reflecting on how we feel when smaller parts—an inflamed toe, for instance, or a ruptured appendix—are in pain.) Each part needs and fully depends on the healthy functioning of all the parts together. Moreover, participation in this body is not optional or voluntary. To think that an individual could be successful alone or solely through individual effort would be like isolating a liver or kidney and believing it could function well by itself.

Paul believes that a desire to stand apart from others, let alone stand against them, is a damaging temptation. This is why he makes the care of each other everyone's most important concern. Everyone needs nurture. Everyone needs help. Belly buttons, mouths, nostrils, ears, and hands that hold are the physical proof of mutual help and support. People must learn the art of genuine sympathy for others. People are to be so intimately bound up with each other, so attuned to each other, that when one person suffers, others don't simply know it but feel it too, and respond with whatever means they have to help. Correlatively, when one person rejoices in a good outcome, others feel the joy too, because another's happiness inspires their own. In a genuinely communal life, the hierarchies that often divide and degrade people are done away with. Differences are affirmed and celebrated because each person has unique gifts that are of value to the whole body.

Love is the crucial power that inspires and animates the organic, communal life that Paul recommends. The love he has in mind, however, is not sentimental or naive. It is the sort of love that is epitomized in the feeding, healing, befriending, and reconciling ministries of Jesus. Reflecting on Jesus's life, Paul distills its qualities as follows: "Love is patient; love is kind; love is not envious or boastful or arrogant or rude. It does not insist on its own way; it is not irritable or resentful; it does not rejoice in wrongdoing, but rejoices in the truth. It bears all things, believes all things, hopes all things, endures all things. Love never ends" (1 Corinthians 13:4–8).[7] This characterization of love signals a way of being in which people's fidelity to and responsibility for each other are the primary concerns. To feel this love is to know that you will not be abandoned, shamed, or abused. It is to know that people will listen to you and come alongside you in ways that facilitate mutual flourishing. This love is genuinely erotic because it immerses people within the creative love of God circulating through every person and every place and because it inspires them to cherish the world they share with each other. Imagine how the feel of life would change if people knew that they were surrounded by, and participating in, this sort of love. What desires and expectations for the future would people have if they felt this love every day?

The challenges and possibilities of a genuinely communal and love-animated life became especially clear to me several years ago when Mark and his family moved to town.[8] Mark had just joined the faculty at the college where I taught, and I was pleased to meet him. He also joined our church, and we were becoming friends. His life, however, took an abrupt turn when his years-long nagging cough became so severe that he had difficulty crossing a room. He coughed up blood. His doctors soon gave him a lung cancer diagnosis and informed him that he had a short time to live. They told Mark that he should prepare his family for his death.

The news was devastating. Having been in our community for only a few months, we all began to worry about how he and his family were going to endure the journey ahead. Who would help navigate all the doctor visits? Who would do the shopping, driving, cooking, and cleaning now that Mark was unable to help? Who would stand alongside his wife and kids as they struggled to cope physically and emotionally with this situation? Who would stay with Mark while family members were at work or in school?

Remarkably, many people pitched in to help. Some brought food. Some bought gift cards. Others volunteered to drop off and pick up the kids at school. Others drove Mark to an unending number of doctor visits. Some sat with Mark during the day so he would not have to be alone. People who barely knew

Mark and his family now adopted them as if that family were their own family. It was beautiful to see this congregation surround Mark and his family with their love, but it was also hard because we knew that our love was hardly perfect. We worried we might say or do something unhelpful or stupid. It was easy to feel inconvenienced by, and sometimes even resentful of, the many needs presented to us. We knew we could be petty and selfish and thus hardly worthy of the call to minister to this family. Seeing Mark's family grieve and endure many ups and downs, watching a man slowly die, knowing that our efforts to help seemed insufficient—it was a lot to bear.

Not long before his death, Mark stood before our congregation and read from a journal entry written several years before. He recorded that his life was a living hell. He was empty and anxious. He disliked everything about his life, his town, his house, and his former job. He described how terribly alone he felt: getting up in the morning filled him with dread. He didn't feel his life mattered. He felt abandoned by God and became an atheist. It was painful to us to hear him describe himself as sullen, withdrawn, angry, and sad.

Mark knew he needed help. Some of it came from a psychiatrist who helped him understand and treat his depression. But he also knew that he needed a new context and new work. That is why he placed so much hope in a new teaching position. We expected to hear that the cancer diagnosis destroyed his hope, but instead he said—oxygen tank tucked under one arm—that now was the best he had felt in years. Mark said he wanted to bear witness to a miracle made evident in his life. He was no longer anxious or lonely. He wasn't sullen or angry. Instead, he felt himself to be surrounded by a thousand arms of love from people he hardly knew, yet who wanted the best for him and his family. This love inspired him to give himself to his family and friends in ways he had scarcely thought possible. He expressed his gratitude for the prayers, food, cards, and the assurances that he was not alone and that others would be there for his family when he was gone. He said that the love he experienced over the last months allowed him to taste the joy of God's kingdom.

As Mark sat down, many of us were weeping. We were deeply moved by his testimony to the transformative power of love. Mark taught us that when love is active, a person can move from feeling alone, worthless, and unforgiven to being a beloved spouse, father, and friend. He taught us that someone who is visibly dying and suffering can be a source of encouragement and hope to others. He taught us that an ugly cancer need not be an obstacle to living a life that is still beautiful and worthy of being cherished.

Love is crucial to a hopeful life because love is the power that creates a welcoming and nurturing community in which people can dream, explore, and develop the potential that is uniquely theirs. Love is paramount because it inspires the "braided dance" in which people can feel themselves moving with each other into the fullness of their particular lives. As Paul says, "And now faith, hope, and love abide, these three; and the greatest of these is love" (1 Corinthians 13:13). Paul believes the call to love is ultimately a call to people to participate in the divine love that daily creates and sustains the universe and all of its life. In other words, the whole of reality functions best when it is animated by the sacred—and divinely erotic—power that nurtures and celebrates life, the sort of power that is evident in the striking profusion, vitality, and diversity of the life we perceive around us. Of course, the world is not without pain and loss, which is why it is all the more important for people to learn to be a nurturing and hospitable presence wherever they are. Even so, love is the action that creates the social and economic contexts in which life has the best chance to thrive. Without love, the world literally falls apart.

Can this divine love be trusted? Paul thinks it can, because it is the form of love that created the universe, that daily nurtures and heals it, and that—in the resurrection of Jesus from the dead—proved itself to be more powerful than violence and abuse. Paul believes that the love of God made incarnate in the person of Jesus is the key that unlocks the meaning and purpose of life. He believes it is the inspiration and the power that animates authentic hope.

James Baldwin had good reasons to be suspicious. The history of Christianity is punctuated by the unspeakably cruel things Christians have done to each other and to outsiders, quite often in the name of Jesus. Their actions seemed to reflect the violent imperial power of the Rome that crucified Jesus, rather than the power of God that is made manifest in what Paul called the "fruit of the Spirit"—love, joy, peace, patience, kindness, generosity, faithfulness, gentleness, and self-control (Galatians 5:22–23).

Baldwin came to his conclusions as someone who saw how love can be perverted. In his "Letter from a Region in My Mind," first published in 1962 in the *New Yorker* and then reprinted the next year in his book *The Fire Next Time,* Baldwin described how he was drawn to life in the Black church: the place that might save him from a life of drugs, despair, and crime. He even became a young minister. Being a preacher was exciting. So much power and pathos were often on display in church services. Moreover, the mantle of the preacher gave him something to be and a position of respect within his community.

But Baldwin's faith soon crumbled. The more he read and reflected, and the more he saw what was happening in congregational life, the more convinced he became that hatred, fear, and hypocrisy had become Christianity's defining powers. The histories of conquest, genocide, slavery, the Holocaust, and Jim Crow testified to the entrenched Christianity-sanctioned hatred that destroyed millions of lives. More locally, there was also the hypocrisy that daily hurt and excluded neighbors. As Baldwin looked around, he concluded, "There was no love in the church. It was a mask for hatred and self-hatred and despair. The transfiguring power of the Holy Ghost ended when the service ended . . . the passion with which we loved the Lord was a measure of how deeply we feared and distrusted and, in the end, hated almost all strangers, always, and avoided and despised ourselves."[9]

Baldwin believed that Christianity, specifically the white God of American Christianity, operated on the principle of fear and thus prevented people from knowing how to love themselves and each other. It had become a gnostic, discarnate faith that elevated the individual soul above everything else, thereby giving people the excuse to ignore and even deride the concerns of their and others' bodies. In despising the flesh of this world, these Christians also destroyed the erotic power that Lorde understood to be fundamental to anyone's flourishing. As Baldwin saw it, white Christians were terrified of sensuality and therefore unable to embrace their embodiment through acts of nurture, healing, and loving touch. This way of living was in striking contrast to the way Jesus lived. "To be sensual," Baldwin said, "is to respect and rejoice in the force of life, of life itself, and to be *present* in all that one does, from the effort of loving to the breaking of bread." Moreover, "if the concept of God has any validity or any use, it can only be to make us larger, freer, and more loving. If God cannot do this, then it is time we got rid of Him."[10]

The lovelessness that Baldwin saw in churches was of a piece with the lovelessness evident in American culture more broadly. Looking at neighborhoods, schools, prisons, and shopping malls, Baldwin saw the signs of a culture trapped in dishonesty, superficiality, loneliness, apathy, and neglect. Too many children were forsaken and unloved. Too many places were abandoned and abused. People were suspicious of each other, constantly afraid that they didn't have enough or that what they had would be taken away from them. They were anxious for themselves because they sensed that money mattered more than people, and they felt that neither they nor their homes were worthy of cherishing. "Everyone is rushing, God knows where, and everyone is looking for God knows what—but it is clear that no one is happy here, and that something is lost."[11] The proof? You look in vain to find people singing for joy, even occasionally, or spontaneously erupting in praise and gratitude for their place and community.

Baldwin understood that people don't live honestly with themselves or with each other. "We are afraid to reveal ourselves because we trust ourselves so little . . . Therefore, the truth cannot be told, even about one's attitudes: we live by lies."[12] People prefer to believe the comforting stories they tell about themselves, stories that position them as either the victors or the victims of fate but not as the perpetrators of injustice and pain. Baldwin knew it was hard to face the exclusion, violence, and murder that have been and are still being committed under the banner of American Christianity.[13] The difficulty of facing exclusion and pain makes the recovery and refinement of love all the more important, because genuine love removes the masks we use to hide from ourselves and each other the truth of who we really are and what we have done. This genuine love is difficult and painful to practice because it depends on people seeing that their ideas of salvation are, often and in fact, versions of hell.

In one of his last essays, Baldwin affirmed that salvation

"is not precipitated by the terror of being consumed in hell: this terror itself places one in hell. Salvation is preceded by the recognition of sin, by conviction, by repentance . . . Salvation is not flight from the wrath of God; it is accepting and reciprocating the love of God. Salvation is not separation. It is the beginning of union with all that is or has been or ever will be." Then again: "There is absolutely no salvation without love: this is the wheel in the middle of the wheel. Salvation does not divide. Salvation connects, so that one sees oneself in others and others in oneself."[14] Love is the essential, erotic power that animates hope because it inspires people to join hands and commit to being a listening, nurturing, and celebrating presence to each other. In a manner similar to Carmine Menna's, Baldwin realized, "The moment we cease to hold each other, the moment we break faith with one another, the sea engulfs us and the light goes out."[15]

Throughout his life Baldwin struggled with hope because he realized how difficult it is for people to love themselves and each other, especially in economic and political contexts driven by fear and hate. He believed that hope evaporates if it is not nurtured by communities of love. But he also believed that if people allowed themselves to be transformed by love, the feel and the meaning of life would be different. If Baldwin is correct in his diagnosis, and I think that he is, then the better question to ask about hope is not "What gives you hope?"—the question we started out with—but "Who and what and how do you love?"

2
When Hope Languishes

When my parents were coming into adulthood in the early 1940s, they were determined not to have children. Like millions of Europeans, they had to flee their homes or risk being shot, bombed, raped, or sent to a work camp to die. There was no escape to safety because there were no safe places to escape to. They were in a "total war" in which the aim of both Allied and Axis powers was domicide, the complete destruction of homes and civilian life. Never before had people seen such desolation. By the war's end, forty-five million people living in Germany and central Europe were homeless. Having witnessed unspeakable brutality and rampant violence, my parents had given up hope in humanity. They couldn't imagine a future that was worth bringing children into.

My mother, Ingrid, grew up on a farm in Poland. Her family was among the millions of Germans who over previous generations had settled in the east, beyond the Oder River, in Poland, Silesia, East Prussia, and Ukraine. Like other small-scale farmers, they raised a few cattle and draft horses, a milk cow, chickens, and pigs and maintained a vegetable garden and a fruit orchard to supply their immediate needs. My mother was happy living there. She went to school, had good friends, loved to run, and enjoyed working with her father, Wilhelm. Though not a luxurious or even an easy life, her family had what they needed, were surrounded by a supportive community, and had time to enjoy the blessings of their farm and their labors.

My mother's world was turned upside down when Adolf Hitler invaded Poland in September 1939. Not long thereafter, Wilhelm was conscripted into the German army and sent to southern France, where he was soon captured by American paratroopers. He was not reunited with his family until after the war, when he returned from a prisoner-of-war camp in Fort Benning, Georgia. Being hundreds and then thousands of miles away, Wilhelm could not have imagined the chaos and brutality that came down on his wife and three children.

The treatment of Poles by German soldiers moving east was horrific. Polish citizens, many of them Jews, were summarily executed or deported so that their homes and farmlands could be appropriated to satisfy Hitler's lust for *Lebensraum*. The atrocities escalated in 1944 when German troops, now in retreat from a Russian army, looted, burned, raped, and executed their way back to their homeland. Hitler wanted the Red Army to find nothing of value as they made their advance to Berlin. The German civilians that remained in Poland now faced the vengeance of both Poles and Russians determined to make Germans pay for the brutality of Hitler's army. The historian Tony Judt summarized the situation: "The Germans had done terrible things to Russia; now it was their turn to suffer. Their possessions and their women were there for the taking. With the tacit consent of its commanders, the Red Army was turned loose on the civilian populations of the newly conquered German lands."[1]

I have not been able to get precise details of all that my mother experienced in those horrid months. She couldn't speak about it. When I asked my dad what happened to her in Poland, he often cried. He said that as best as he could piece things together, my mother, along with all the other grandmas, mothers, and young women, was likely assaulted and raped by Russian soldiers. In her village, nights were punctuated by the shrieking of women trying to fend off their attackers. Children were hidden under beds or in fields or were made to look as hideous and smell as foully as possible, all in an often futile attempt to repulse the advances of soldiers. My mother was among the "lucky" ones who survived. Thousands of women in Poland were raped, stabbed, mutilated, or shot and then left strewn about, hung on doors, or even crucified on church altars.

The rape of women has long been a feature of warfare. But during World War II the number of rapes across Europe was staggering, with as many as 2,000,000 German women raped in the war's aftermath (100,000 in Berlin alone). The details of living conditions in central Europe have come to light only in recent decades as formerly closed Soviet archives have opened. The current estimate is that between 150,000 and 200,000 "Russian babies" were born in Soviet-occupied German lands in 1945–46. This number does not include the untold number of abortions carried out by German women who despised their plight. Nor does it include the many women who died in an abortion attempt. Among the women who could be interviewed, some reported that they were raped by gangs of Russian soldiers as many as sixty to seventy times per day. Many of the children born during this period were a daily reminder of atrocity. The women who survived months of violation, hunger, disease, and deprivation had to carry on in states of fear, anger, anxiety, and self-loathing. Many took their own lives.

My father Alex's family had farmed for a time outside Kiev, but when their land was confiscated by the government, they moved north, eventually settling in East Prussia, where my paternal grandfather, August, worked for a farmer. In 1940 August was conscripted into the German army and sent to Lithuania to work as a customs official. He was not reunited with his family until December 31, 1945, at which time he learned of the deaths of three of his older children. My dad, age nine when his father left for Lithuania, was the oldest of the siblings to stay home. Care for his sickly mother and his three younger brothers fell on him. At age thirteen, my dad made the decision to burn the family's identification papers for fear that they might all be sent to Siberia to die in the Gulag (the fate of his older sister). He also made the decision in the spring of 1944 for the family to flee westward in hopes of evading an advancing and widely feared Russian army. The American diplomat George Kennan later wrote in his memoirs, "The disaster that befell this area with the entry of the Soviet forces has no parallel in modern European existence. There were considerable sections of it where, to judge by all existing evidence, scarcely a man, woman or child of the indigenous population was left alive."[2]

The journey west was dangerous and cruel. Perpetually hungry and terrified, my father spent most of every day scavenging for food and finding places for his mother and his siblings to rest. The scale of the destruction they encountered along the way is hard to describe. Buildings in villages and towns were reduced to rubble. Fields and farms were burned to the ground. The smell of dead animals and dead people was everywhere. They eventually settled for a short while on a farm in Poland in the early months of 1945.

While there, one of my dad's tasks was to bury the corpses that were rotting in ditches and fields. One particularly warm spring afternoon, after a grueling day of burying livestock, my dad asked his mom if he and his companion could go for a swim in a pond nearby. She said he needed to get on with several farm chores first. That decision, though infuriating at the time, saved my dad's life. As his companion walked away, his shovel, now deployed as a walking stick, hit a landmine. My dad fell to the ground, but not before being pelted with pieces of this boy's flesh.

By the end of the summer of 1945, it became clear that my dad and his family could not stay in Poland. In the middle of the night, they managed to board a train bound for Berlin. That first night, however, bandits assaulted them and took the little money and food they had managed to scrape together. They also took my father's shoes (which he went without until January 1946, thereby permanently damaging his feet). Upon arriving in East Berlin, they were overwhelmed to see the city's destruction. Hardly a building had escaped the Allied bombs and fires that left many German cities in ruins. General Eisenhower had been clear that he wanted to bomb Germany into oblivion. He remarked: "City after city has been systematically shattered. Our artillery could scarcely add to the completeness of the material destruction."[3]

As a child, I often heard my parents say they had thought the world was literally coming to an end. Wherever they looked, they saw destruction and desolation, rape and ruin. The land itself had become dangerous, a site of death rather than life. Strangers invariably aroused suspicion and fear. Years later, after reading the accounts of historians, I have come to appreciate that my parents were trying to imagine their future in conditions of complete economic, social, psychic, and spiritual collapse. The journalist Anne O'Hare McCormick, writing for the *New York Times* in March 1945, put the matter plainly: "The human problem the war will leave behind it has not yet been imagined, much less faced by anybody. There has never been such destruction, such disintegration of the structure of life."[4]

The despair and desperation my parents must have felt is hard for me to imagine. Beyond the immense physical destruction everywhere around, and the perpetual danger of vigilantes and unexploded mines and artillery, they also had to face the utter collapse of the social networks and institutions that give personal life stability and meaning. Families were in tatters. Young children walked aimlessly about, looking for their parents.[5] Severe hunger reduced people to marauding animals who would slit another's throat or offer up their own bodies to get a morsel of food. Theft was rampant. Violence was a regular feature of daily life. Civic and legal rights ceased to exist. In this world, trust—in authority, policies, and people—had evaporated. The summer and fall of 1945 was not the birth of a new Europe rising out of the ashes of war. It was, instead, a descent into anguish and anarchy. Writing in 1947, the US undersecretary of state Dean Acheson said, "We could see the physical destruction but the effect of vast economic disruption and political, social, and psychological destruction . . . completely escaped us."[6]

My parents did eventually have four children because their world and their circumstances had changed dramatically. In the early 1950s my mother and father emigrated to western Canada with their families, and there, despite significant hardship, they also found a welcoming community that provided solace and support. Unlike West Germany, where refugees from central Europe were unwelcome and opportunities virtually nonexistent, Alberta offered meaningful work, stable institutions, a relatively safe home, and a chance to start life over. That was enough to convince my parents to marry and raise a family. I would not have been born had there not been the prospect of a new, safe beginning.

Untold millions of people have existed and continue to exist in places defined by brutality, oppression, and neglect. Warfare, slavery, worker abuse, domestic violence, rape, displacement, incarceration, eviction, prejudice, alienation—these are just some of the conditions that have for centuries defined the day-to-day living of far too many people. In addition to these social calamities, there are the "natural" calamities of hunger, illness, and familial death that make many people orphans, widows or widowers, or refugees. As recently as the start of the nineteenth century, the average life expectancy at birth for the world population "was at most thirty years; only exceptionally did it rise to thirty-five or a little higher. More than half of all people died before reaching adulthood."[7]

The vast majority of these people who never reached adulthood are unknown to us, having slipped into the oblivion of times past. Nonetheless, the testimonies of the relatively few who left records of their abuse and suffering remind us that each person who enters the world embodies life's specific, never-again-to-be-repeated potential. These records help us appreciate what an injustice and tragedy it is that so many people never had the chance to explore and achieve the life that was uniquely theirs. Caught in a grim present, and with a dim future ahead, great numbers of people had little prospect of a hopeful life. For too many people, that is still true today.

People need to experience nurture and support if they are to live in a hopeful manner. They need to know that their natural worlds are healthy and fertile, that their neighborhoods are welcoming and safe, and that the moral and spiritual ideals of their communities are praiseworthy and good. People need homes and places of learning in which they can dream and pursue life's possibilities. One of the best ways to measure the health of a culture, therefore, is by how it treats its young people and how it forms them to care about their society's future.

In a wide-ranging study, *Juvenescence,* Robert Pogue Harrison suggests that human growth is like a tree's: deep roots extend back into the past to find nurture and wisdom, and branches extend toward the sunlight to find an open and potentially fruitful future. This characterization makes it clear that one of the most important functions of a society is to confer on the young the sense that they are heirs of the past rather than orphans. As heirs, they can receive and renew the legacies of forebears because they recognize the good in them, however imperfect these legacies may be. But as orphans, they see the past as alien, repulsive, even hostile, and so dissociate themselves from it. The tragedy of so much modern history is that young people feel themselves to be orphans in time. They want little to do with histories that are saturated with abuse, abandonment, and violence. When they look to the future, the prospects are diminished and dim. The result? They lose the *amor mundi,* the love for the world, that takes custody of, and assumes responsibility for, its future. "For the world to last *as a world,* and not merely as a habitat," Harrison argues, "those who live in it must continue to consider it their own. Once it becomes alien to them, or once they sense it is no longer *their* world, they withdraw their love from it. This shedding of *amor mundi* is the biggest danger the world faces today, for the *mundus* disappears along with the *amor* that took custody of its future."[8]

A growing number of young people feel that their leaders do not care very much about the world they and the next generations will inherit. Accordingly, they report that they are seriously contemplating, and sometimes deciding, not to have children. Scholars are just beginning to turn their attention to Birthstrikers and GINKs (Green Inclination, No Kids), now estimated to number at about 12.5 million in the United States. In one study, conducted with 607 (mostly white, mostly college- and graduate-school-educated) Americans who are factoring climate change into their reproductive decision-making, 60 percent expressed serious concern about the carbon footprint of each new child, while 96 percent were very concerned about the expected quality of life and well-being of existing and yet-to-be-born children. Most respondents believed the future to be bleak, with extreme heat, flooding, wars over dwindling resources, mass starvation, and large-scale migration of climate refugees being some of its defining features.[9]

In a more recent, expansive, and diverse study (conducted with 10,000 young people aged sixteen to twenty-five, representing ten countries [the United Kingdom, France, Norway, Portugal, Brazil, India, the United States, the Philippines, Nigeria, and Australia]), 83 percent said people have failed to care for the planet, 75 percent said the future is frightening, 56 percent felt that humanity is doomed, and nearly 40 percent said they are hesitant to have children. A total of 65 percent said governments are failing young people and are lying about their efforts to work for a better future. The majority felt betrayed by society's leaders and have grown cynical in response to the hypocrisy they see about them. In almost every category, the percentage went up for young people living in poorer countries.[10] The range of emotions that young people felt varied, but they were overwhelmingly negative. Fear, sadness, anxiety, anger, powerlessness, grief, depression, and guilt were some of the most common.

The context for many of these young people is not, as it was for my parents, a world war. It is the reality of climate change, which some environmental activists characterize as a war against the natural world itself. For these young people the climate crisis is not a far-off possibility but a present and existential threat that is closing the windows on their future prospects. For them, dreams have been replaced by nightmares. Young people feel ignored, abandoned, and betrayed by the adults charged with their care, which is why they are marching, striking from schools, and turning to the courts to protect the planet that scientists are telling us is becoming increasingly uninhabitable. They are doing this because they know that children, especially those living in poorer countries, will bear the brunt of climate catastrophes. A recent report by UNICEF says that one billion children are already at "extremely high risk" from the effects of pollution and climate change and that a future with intensifying heat waves, floods, fires, disease, and drought is "unimaginably dire."[11]

Greta Thunberg speaks for many young people when she says that adult leaders cannot be believed when they say that they love their children. Pointing to years of deflection, lies, subterfuge, hypocrisy, and inaction on the part of business and government officials, Thunberg argues, "If the adults really loved us they would at least do everything they possibly could to make sure we have a safe future, a future to look forward to. But they are not doing that. As it is now it feels like they are doing the exact opposite."[12] To make her case, Thunberg points again and again to the findings of the Intergovernmental Panel on Climate Change (IPCC). This international body draws on the latest and best scientific data available to describe what is happening on earth, what the key drivers are, and what future scenarios are likely, based on various rates of temperature increase.

The 2023 IPCC Assessment Report, in its Summary Statement to Policymakers, does not mince words: "It is unequivocal that human influence has warmed the atmosphere, ocean and land" and that "human well-being and planetary health are under threat."[13] The earth is warming at an unprecedented rate, with carbon dioxide concentration levels in the atmosphere being higher in 2019 than they have been in at least two million years. Moreover, we are fast approaching tipping points—like the melting of the permafrost, which releases methane (a heat-trapping gas more potent than carbon dioxide) into the atmosphere—that will lock in warming rates no matter what people do now.

Thunberg says repeatedly that our civilization must change and that political economies can no longer operate by the same rules as they have been. Indeed, according to the IPCC report, unless the wealthy people of this world make a drastic shift in the way they live, we can expect to see global temperatures increase by at least 2–2.5 degrees Celsius by century's end. The last time planet earth was this warm was over three million years ago, long before *Homo sapiens* made its home here.

The material effects of a warming planet are enormous and wide-ranging:

- more frequent and intense heat waves
- more extreme weather events—torrential rains, hurricanes, tornadoes, cyclones, dust storms—that precipitate flooding and/or drought
- an increase in the frequency and intensity of forest fires
- the reduction, even elimination, of glaciers and mountain snowpacks that provide fresh water to millions of people
- the unsustainable drawdown of aquifers to irrigate food and commodity crops
- rising sea levels owing to the melting of on-land ice sheets (especially in Greenland and Antarctica) and the expansion of water as it warms
- the extinction of untold microbial, insect, plant, animal, and fish species owing to the disruption of land and ocean ecosystems

Taken individually, even one of these effects is enough to impair the flourishing of communities in particular regions of the world. Taken together, however, they create the conditions for horrific levels of misery. Consider some of the following scenarios:

- Multiple megacities that lack an energy and cooling infrastructure overheat, causing millions to flee (where?) for months of the year or evacuate permanently.
- Freshwater shortages create civil unrest and cross-state, cross-country conflict.
- Food production plummets owing to catastrophic weather events (drought, flooding, untimely frost cycles) and the loss of pollinator species.
- Heat endangers the lives of millions of outdoor manual workers.
- Agricultural production and fisheries collapse, creating the conditions for mass starvation.
- Coastal cities and communities flood, creating massive housing and infrastructure crises.
- The creation and movement of tens of millions of "climate refugees" ignites widespread xenophobia and political unrest.
- Fierce conflicts erupt over the ownership of energy and mineral resources.

Current headlines about drought, record-breaking heat, floods, forest fires, calving icebergs, failed crops, and on and on, tell us that such events are already in train. Indeed, let us recognize that so far IPCC reports have sometimes *under*estimated the speed and the seriousness of several of the effects coming our way. The oft-repeated claims that "technology will solve this" or "it is too expensive to make the changes we need to make" must be dismissed. Those who make such statements simply do not grasp the seriousness or the urgency of our situation. Thunberg routinely chides world leaders to grow up, face the truth of our situation, and act responsibly—that is, as if the lives of children and grandchildren really matter. False, sentimental, and cynical hope needs to come to an end. Speaking to some of the world's most powerful people in Davos in 2019, Thunberg said, "Adults keep saying: 'We owe it to the young people to give them hope.' But I don't want your hope. I don't want you to be hopeful. I want you to panic. I want you to feel the fear I feel every day. And I want you to act. I want you to act as you would in a crisis. I want you to act as if our house is on fire. Because it is."[14]

3
Resonant Hope

When Anna Wiener moved to Silicon Valley, she knew she was entering the "promised land" for people working in the high-tech, big-data economy. With a six-figure salary and possible stock options on the horizon, why struggle in New York City to make ends meet, working in publishing houses that were shrinking their staffs, salaries, and benefits? Besides, the lure and promise of big data were compelling. "Not everyone knew what they needed from big data, but everyone knew that they needed it. Just the prospect incited lust in product managers, advertising executives, and stock market speculators . . . Investors salivated over predictive analytics, the lucrative potential of steroidal pattern-matching, and the prospect of bringing machine-learning algorithms to the masses." Silicon Valley exuded optimism, "the optimism of no hurdles, no limits, no bad ideas. The optimism of capital, power, and opportunity."[1] It seemed like the place to be.

Wiener was aware that the industry wasn't all golden. She wished, for instance, that data companies were more transparent about how they planned to use (and sell) the mountains of data they were collecting, and more transparent about how they collected it. She was impressed—and increasingly distressed—

by the technologies that had been developed to capture information about people at the most granular (and private) levels, technologies that were able to track almost any person's age, gender, political affiliation, diet, weight, health, income, favorite movies and books, travel interests, education, work schedules and performance, recreational pursuits, and shopping and eating preferences (to name a few of the data categories). If people connected online or used a cell phone, they were in the system, whether they knew it or not. It seemed obvious that the lives of people would be "improved" if they used the digital devices and networks that were creating "smart" homes, workplaces, and cities. Why should people put their health needs in the hands of fallible and finite doctors when they could upload their medical histories and bio-profiles to a digital platform where sophisticated algorithms could access all the world's medical knowledge and give the most accurate diagnoses possible? Why not choose the precision, reliability, and power of machines over people, however expert, who are regularly stressed, get tired or distracted, and make mistakes? Why not use ChatGPT or some other app to help you present your "best self" to others?

But the longer Wiener worked and the more she saw, the more unsettled she became. Almost every customer she met was guided by the same North Star: "whatever brought in money—as much of that as possible." The endgame of nearly every start-up was the fastest growth possible, at any cost. The aim was to disrupt existing markets and then find a way to dominate them. Companies wanted a "world of actionable metrics, in which developers would never stop optimizing and users would never stop looking at their screens. A world freed of decision-making, the unnecessary friction of human behavior, where everything—whittled down to the fastest, simplest, sleekest versions of itself—could be optimized, prioritized, monetized, and controlled."[2] Under the banner of unmatched availability of products, services, and experiences, designers were making it harder and harder for consumers to abandon their shopping carts. With the mantra of improved performance, companies were creating digital dependency and profound personal restlessness: restlessness for more, and a restlessness for something new and different.

It was also clear to Wiener that the services and products sold by Silicon Valley companies were changing people. "Everyone I knew was stuck in a feedback loop with themselves. Technology companies stood by, ready to become everyone's library, memory, personality. I read whatever the other nodes in my social network were reading. I listened to whatever music the algorithms told me to. Wherever I traveled on the internet, I saw my own data reflected back to me." But whose data was it really? Her mind was constantly being addressed, even assaulted, by the thoughts and feelings of others (or bots). Were the thoughts and desires she had truly her own? Submitting to social and media networks was immersing her in a world where people seemed desperate to stand out and prove that they mattered. In addition to all the anger and rage she encountered, there was much more: a steady stream of people baring their souls, revealing their every emotion, thought, and movement, begging to be noticed. "People were giving themselves away at every opportunity."[3] Silicon Valley was creating a world of unceasing self-expression and self-promotion in search of meaningful connections with others.

And yet so many of these efforts were coming up short. Why?

To understand the ethos and ambition of Silicon Valley companies, it helps to have two historical trajectories in view. The first follows the history of California. As Malcolm Harris has recently narrated that history, California is both a state and a state of mind where several of the animating impulses of modernity came together. "The scientific principles of control, measurement, and deliberate change opened a road to modernity, and capital was the draft mule that pulled the whole world down that path, California first."[4]

The pursuit of wealth was and is the beating heart of many of the projects that lured settlers and investors to California. The rush for gold, the violent appropriation of land from Indigenous peoples, the engineering of technologies to mine and farm the land, the promise of a cheap and (legally) powerless workforce, the transformation of land (that grows plants) into real estate (that grows profits), the deployment of stock market logics and corporate consolidation to develop railroads and massive infrastructure projects—these are some of the strategies that were refined on America's west coast. The founding of Stanford University in 1885 created the quintessential center for the financial investment, scientific research, and economic development that would define Silicon Valley's culture and catapult several individuals to the heights of extreme wealth (Leland Stanford, Herbert Hoover, William Hewlett, David Packard, Steve Jobs, Bill Gates, Larry Page, Mark Zuckerberg, Travis Kalanick, Jeff Bezos, and Peter Thiel are among the most famous).

Given this historical context of ambition, the invention of the internet was like the arrival of the Messiah. By promising unlimited connections on multiple networks, companies could gain access to multitudes of "users," stimulate consumer desires, and monetize their connections. All that was needed to lure investors was a promising idea that inspired confidence. That idea would lure the second round of investors, jack up the price of the company's stocks, and make paper millionaires. Investors were especially attracted to companies capable of creating new markets that disrupted traditional industries: they funded streaming services that bypassed movie theaters, online retailers that rendered local businesses obsolete, and ride-sharing platforms that circumvented taxi service regulations. "A merely profitable business wasn't good enough; if you wanted capital, you had to scale, which made every enterprise into a binary bet. These firms needed their employees to *win,* to do whatever needed to be done, to outcompete teams of hundreds of workers, to replace whole workforces."[5]

David Jordan, the university president who shaped Stanford at its founding, played a key role in engineering the culture of innovation and domination that business demanded. Jordan championed "bionomics" because he believed it to be the science that would enable society's (mostly white, mostly male) leaders to identify and properly educate the high IQ workforce that would create advancement and wealth, the kind of workforce that would dominate competitors.[6] On Harris's reading, Silicon Valley rests on an educational ethos obsessed with competition and acquisition. "The model is progress by victory, defeat, and ruthless elimination, full speed from day one. It is the Palo Alto system . . . It's impersonal: forces, not men. Someone's going to go to Stanford. Someone's going to make billions of dollars. Palo Alto exists to find and develop them early, as soon as possible."[7]

In an op-ed in the *Palo Alto Weekly,* Carolyn Walworth, a junior at Palo Alto High School and a student representative on the school board, made clear the personal toll on students that the "Palo Alto system" was taking. "We are not teenagers. We are lifeless bodies in a system that breeds competition, hatred, and discourages teamwork and genuine learning. We lack sincere passion. We are sick . . . It is time to realize that we work our students to death."[8] Walworth meant it literally. The railway line on which Leland Stanford built some of his fortune has become a regular site at which Palo Alto teenagers are committing suicide.

The second historical trajectory that will help us understand Silicon Valley companies centers on the technological development that Silicon Valley has come to represent. As Luke Fernandez and Susan J. Matt have documented, the emotional landscapes, personal styles, and ideas about what constitutes a good human life have regularly changed as new technologies—like the telegraph, telephones, tractors, automobiles, radios, phonographs, household appliances, televisions, computers, and iPhones—are introduced. In previous generations many Americans lived with an understanding of personal limits and constraints and with the knowledge that hardship and monotony were inescapable parts of a human life. People expected their social worlds to be fairly small and the geographies of their lives to be circumscribed.

By the early twenty-first century these assumptions had evaporated. Technologically enabled individuals found "new ways of expressing, amusing, and projecting themselves—ways that seem to give them new capacities." Older notions of what it means to be human no longer seemed to apply. People came to believe that "it is possible to have few constraints on their online identities, on their modes of expression, on their social connections." In fact, Americans now "increasingly believe that they can have easy and infinite social connections, endless diversion and stimulation, unceasing affirmation of their worth, and boundless intellectual capacity." Life can be many things, but it shouldn't ever be boring: that's the current mindset. Anything less than an unbounded life and an unlimited self now feels like an unwarranted diminishment of human potential. To be emotionally fulfilled means "never being lonely, always being engaged and affirmed by others, being unconstrained in anger, and able to multi-task and apprehend everything."[9]

This (very brief) look at the recent history of technological development helps us appreciate that technological devices are never simply "tools" that leave people more or less unchanged. They have the power to transform human feelings and desires, bestow new personal identities, and create new avenues for engagement—and thereby also alter what people expect from life and from each other.

Smartphones are a prime example of what I mean. One reason these devices are so alluring is that they promise uninterrupted connection with others. No matter where you are—provided you have cell service!—you can reach out and be reached. They also promise unlimited and immediate access to every place, every event, every person, every artifact, every creature, every commodity, and every piece of information available. Previous generations would have thought it impossible for anyone to have the whole world in the palm of a hand, but today the impossibility lies in imagining daily life without a smartphone. To lose it is like losing the bodily appendage that gives you a hold on life and all that the world has to offer (and sell).

There is more than one way to approach and hold on to life. Think here of the difference between a caress, a handshake, a punch, a grab, and an embrace. These gestures presuppose vastly different ways of approaching life, but they also communicate differing assumptions about the kind of world we are in and what humanity's place within it ought to be. Smartphones help us do many things. They can, for instance, give people unending streams of entertainment; connect people across vast distances; reduce creatures and places to commodities easily and always available for purchase; introduce people to cultures and histories they would otherwise never know; give people the impression that they can have life on their own terms. Have these uses helped us clarify what the goal and point of a human life ought to be? In some cases, they clearly have. But has the technological matrix in which smartphones operate also given us a false hope, a set of expectations and desires that regularly frustrate us and keep us feeling alone and unsatisfied?

The proliferation of laptops, tablets, and smartphones, the invention of social media platforms like Facebook, Instagram, TikTok, and X (formerly Twitter), and the profusion of apps to streamline and make almost every task easier indicate that the opportunities to "connect," "express," and "achieve" are endless. These developments aren't all bad. But something isn't working. Though loneliness industries have developed that teach people to expect that "happy, sociable fulfillment is easy, always possible, and the norm," people still feel lost, alone, and exhausted.[10]

When thinking about the "promised land" that Silicon Valley has created, two facts need to be kept in view. First, Silicon Valley has given people access to nearly everything the world has to offer, and with an ease that would have been unimaginable to the most wealthy and powerful people of previous generations. Second, access isn't enough. People still want more, they want different, and they want it now. Why the lack of contentment?

In *Resonance: A Sociology of Our Relationship to the World,* the German sociologist Hartmut Rosa argues that there is a paradox at the heart of today's desire to connect, achieve, and acquire: the more people pursue an unbounded life and a limitless self, the more they feel themselves to be discontented and alone. The quest to maximize quantities of connections and stuff has come at the cost of losing the essential qualities that make connections meaningful and satisfying. What's missing in our relationships is the quality that Rosa describes as *resonance.*

Resonance is an acoustic phenomenon best revealed when putting two tuning forks in proximity to each other. When one vibrates, the other responds spontaneously by vibrating along with it. Mutual responsivity, mutual sympathy, mutual attunement—these are the key features of resonant connections. Rosa's aim is not to reduce people to tuning forks. It is, rather, to describe the practical conditions—things like patient listening, gentle care, and abiding mutuality—under which people can be in the presence of each other and feel inspired and freshly alive. When resonance is happening, people are in tune with each other and appreciate that their own well-being is intimately bound up with the well-being of others. They become less restless because they feel the contentment, even the joy, that comes from being in a life-enhancing and life-cherishing relationship.

Everything about people suggests that they are created for resonant relationships. Resonance begins in the womb with a fetus and its mother in constant, rhythmic, visceral communication with each other. It continues after birth in the skin-on-skin contact that communicates welcome, tenderness, and nurture. Much of a person's subsequent life may well be a yearning for the various forms of touch that communicate this foundational, gentle, life-affirming, and life-giving affection. As we grow, breathing and eating provide an especially intimate relationship with the world; we take in but also let out. The relationships are never simply mechanical. Fragrant aromas, delectable flavors, and erotic touch set our bodies alight with arousal and pleasure, heightening our sense of the world's liveliness and loveliness and the suitability of our presence within it.

Hearing and speaking are other elemental and embodied indications of the human need for a responsive relationship with a world saturated with sound, a world in which waves, wind, wrens, wolves, and whales call out to each other and to us. Who hasn't felt the pleasure of a voice that makes the heart leap, a rhythm that generates a dance step, or a melody that brings forth a smile? From the start, our vulnerable and susceptible bodies signal that we need and want relationships that animate and nourish us. Merely to be stimulated is never enough. It is far more necessary to be moved, transformed, and inspired. A paradigmatic resonant relationship for many people is the experience of "falling in love." The ones we love aren't mute or dead. Instead, we feel their being pulsing through our own, empowering us to experience life's gratuitous wonder and mystery.

Silicon Valley and the Palo Alto system do not present us with a wonder- or affection-inspiring world. Instead, they give us a world made endlessly available for commodification, manipulation, and consumption. They do not encourage people to be gentle with and affectionate toward others. Instead, they give us competitors committed to optimizing and maximizing their control over the world. The ways and ambitions of Silicon Valley assume a "scientific/rationalistic understanding of the world [that] is based on a mute relationship to the world in which 'objects' . . . can scarcely be understood to be responsive."[11] The varied efforts to make the world legible and predictable, knowable and accessible, pliable and manageable, and, above all, useful and purchasable create the conditions in which places and things cease to be themselves. What they are is what we want them to be. This instrumental way of relating to others is both aggressive and silencing. It has the effect of reducing others to machinelike objects that are without moral significance and that can therefore exert little moral or affective claim upon us. In the rush to transform living beings into "units" of production or "data" to be fed into an algorithm, the mystery and grace of their being are lost.

The objectionable character of this system becomes apparent the moment we reflect on the fact that no person wants to be treated as a unit or data point in someone else's optimization calculus. The steady, relentless stream of notifications and solicitations coming from anonymous coders, calling centers, algorithms, bots, and corporations communicates a world in which others are mostly interested in getting our attention, especially our money. What people genuinely want, however, is to be welcomed and encouraged as the unique beings that they are, endowed with particular gifts and potential but also with specific challenges and limitations. It takes a lot of attention and patience to be fully present to others, and a lot of love, tenderness, and empathy for people to come into resonant relationships with others.[12]

The magic and the deception of the Palo Alto system is that it tricks us into thinking that we can substitute quality relationships with a quantity of accumulated things, "hits," and "likes." It trains people to fear that they do not have or do enough. This system creates people who are restless, ungrateful, and discontented with what they have, what they have accomplished, where they are, who they are with, and who they themselves are. Caught as they are between media- and marketer-manufactured desires for hyper-optimization and hyper-accumulation, people cannot help but feel inadequate, even depressed; they sense that they have never accomplished *enough.*[13] The crucial thing to note is that fear, anxiety, restlessness, and stress destroy resonance.

Resonance cannot be manufactured or engineered. We can't predict when it will happen, even as we work to create the conditions in which it might. Nor can we orchestrate it to achieve some predetermined end. To try to force resonance is like trying to force another person to love you. The experience of resonance is a gift and a grace. The possibility that we might be touched, moved, and feel more alive depends upon encountering a world that is other, uncontrollable, mysterious, and wonderful. It depends on making ourselves vulnerable before the world. As Rosa describes it, "There must be an aspect of *inherent uncontrollability* not only in our experiences or in our relationship to the world, but also *in things themselves,* if we are to be able to enter into a resonant relationship with them."[14] The moment we try to control others is also the moment when we have lost respect for them, and the moment when they cease to be a source of wonder to us.[15]

The effort to control the world has backfired. We now see multiple environments becoming increasingly unpredictable, dangerous, and uninhabitable. "The uncontrollability generated by processes intended to make the world controllable produce a radical alienation . . . Where 'everything is under control,' the world no longer has anything to say to us, and where it has become newly uncontrollable, we can no longer hear it, because we cannot *reach* it."[16]

Long before the invention of Silicon Valley, the ancient Israelites were being prepared to enter a vastly different Promised Land. In this land the people were to witness a hopeful way of being that honored and cherished life. In it no creature and no place were to be treated as a unit in someone else's optimization plan. Having just been liberated from their enslavement in Egypt, the Israelites knew firsthand what it feels like to be objectified and abused. They saw up close how the drive to control others depends on violence and how the unbridled pursuits of wealth and glory ultimately fail to satisfy. But to live this other way, they were going to have to learn to think about their lives and the point of all their striving in a radically new way. Their instruction took the form of a command from God, a command in which God models a resonant way of relating to the world: "Remember the sabbath day, and keep it holy. Six days you shall labor and do all your work. But the seventh day is a sabbath to the Lord your God; you shall not do any work—you, your son or your daughter, your male or female slave, your livestock, or the alien resident in your towns. For in six days the Lord made heaven and earth, the sea, and all that is in them, but rested the seventh day; therefore the Lord blessed the sabbath day and consecrated it" (Exodus 20:8–11). Why does God say that the key to proper striving is to regularly stop striving? What does God's "resting" on the seventh day teach us about the world we are in and the possibility of a hopeful life?

The context for God's sabbath commandment is Genesis 1–2, the opening passage of scripture that narrates in poetic form the creation of the universe. God's creative work is archetypal and foundational, not only because it results in the proliferation of verdant and beautiful life-forms, but because it makes possible and sets the standard for any subsequent work that people might do. One of the most striking features of God's work is that God regularly pauses to affirm the goodness of what is being created. After creating the land, sky, water, air, plants, birds, fish, animals, and people, we are told, "God saw everything that he had made, and indeed, it was very good" (Genesis 1:31). What makes it good is not only God's affirmation of it. God's work is good and beautiful because it creates the liveliness and loveliness that result in the proliferation and flourishing of creatures. The world God makes is fertile and fecund, capable of diverse and ever-fresh sounds, shapes, smells, colors, sights, and flavors. There is nothing dull or boring about this world. Above all, God does not create this world and its creatures by dominating and controlling them. Instead, God gives creatures the freedom, what we might also describe as the erotic capacity, to become themselves by being in mutually beneficial relations with others and, through their co-becoming, the freedom to generate new life.[17]

A good and beautiful world was finished on the sixth day, but it was not yet fully finished. Why is this a crucial point? Because making in and of itself leaves unanswered the question "Why make anything at all?" In other words, the story of

God creating a world only becomes complete when we understand the reason for its creation. That reason, it turns out, is revealed on the seventh day in God's practice of the first Shabbat, the first time of rest. It is when we consider God's resting on the seventh day that we understand the point and purpose of any and all activity.

Why does God rest? As the narrative flow of the text makes clear, God doesn't rest because he is tired or because he wants a break from the bother of maintaining a freshly made world. When God looks out onto creation on the first sabbath sunrise, God does not see a warehouse or stockpile of commodities that exhaust or frustrate him. Instead, God perceives what his own creative, self-giving love looks, smells, sounds, tastes, and feels like once it has become embodied. No creature simply is. Rather, each creature and every place is God's love variously made visible, fragrant, audible, nutritious, and tactile. The whole of creation is a sacred scene where love, beauty, and goodness are everywhere on display. The last thing God would want to do is to exploit or abandon it. The time of sabbath is the time of delight and joy because that is when people experience being in the presence of shared love. God's rest, in other words, realizes what a resonant relationship at its best looks like. We see God fully in love with the creatures he made, fully affirming their goodness and grace, and fully committed to their flourishing. Fully in tune with creatures, there is no other place God wants to be.

The rest that God models, and the sabbath rest God calls his followers to observe, is not opposed to activity. It is, instead, opposed to all the forms of restlessness that communicate their unhappiness and discontentment with what they have, who they are, what they have accomplished, where they are, and who they are with. When people are restless, they are on a perpetual quest for more, for better, for something or someone else. In their world contentment and satisfaction are always beyond reach. In their world habitats, communities, families, and individuals are steadily degraded and destroyed by the insatiable demands being placed upon them.

Restless people find it impossible to arrive at the moment when they possess or have done enough. What they fail to appreciate is that the quest for an unbounded life creates the conditions in which limits will not be respected, nor will the integrity of creatures escape violation. God's sabbath rest models an entirely different way to think about life and behave in the world. God offers a resonant way of being that welcomes and engages others as sacred gifts to be cherished and celebrated. God's command that the Israelites observe the sabbath every seventh day is, therefore, at root God's call to create the practical conditions in which people might fall in love with each other and with the world they share with fellow creatures.[18] The assumption, of course, is that people are able to experience their world as worthy of their love and then find true contentment in the love they share with others. Is shared love enough?

If hope is a way of life in which people are intimately and practically "joined with all the living," and if hope takes the embodied form of a braided dance in which people come alongside others in the modes of sympathy and celebration, then there is no more important task than to learn the ways of sabbath rest. It is in this rest that people discover how precious life is and how worthy it is of our care and devotion. Sabbath rest is the practical context that prepares people to come appreciatively into the presence of each other to celebrate their goodness and to defend them when they are being violated, exhausted, or abandoned. It creates the time in which people remember that they are created to be in resonant relationships with each other and with their life-giving homes. Sabbath rest is vital to our future hope.

4
Hope Grows in Places of Belonging

When I was growing up on a farm in southern Alberta, I had a strong sense of where I belonged. The Rocky Mountains lined our western horizon, and a vast prairie stretched out into the east. Our sky was immense. On clear days I relished lying down in a field and looking up at the cumulus clouds that sometimes formed overhead. On some days the chinook winds coming through Crowsnest Pass were so strong that it was hard to stand up straight. When the winds calmed down, I often caught the scent of sweetgrass. Our soil was loamy and thick. Earthworms were so abundant that flocks of seagulls had a feast every time they followed our plow across a field. We expected extremes in weather, ranging from blinding blizzards in winter to intense dry heat in summer. One summer afternoon our entire grain crop was demolished by golf-ball-sized hailstones that plummeted down from a nearly black sky.

I am the youngest in a family with four kids that raised chickens, pigs, and cattle and grew alfalfa, barley, wheat, and oats. We also tended a large garden of potatoes, carrots, peas, beans, spinach, cauliflower, peppers, and onions. Almost every day was shaped by what plants, animals, and the farm itself needed. There were many chores: livestock to feed, eggs to gather, fields to plow, seed, and irrigate, hay to mow, a cow to milk, buildings and machinery to maintain, garden plots to weed, and crops to harvest. From an early age I was made to understand that the world does not revolve around me. I was taught that the success of our family depended on the health and vitality of the farm, which is why farmwork defined our days.

All this labor amounted to much more than a job. The daily rounds of chores and responsibilities had the effect of *placing* me in our farm. The work both anchored me in this particular region, like roots that spread out in multiple directions, and nurtured me by giving me food, shelter, and a purpose. The farm provided me with an identity, an orientation, and a vocation to explore and live into. By giving me a schedule of work to do, the farm also initiated me into a way of being that helped me see life as a complex, vulnerable, and integrated reality in which creatures of all kinds depend on each other for whatever flourishing they might achieve.

I did not always welcome the work. On many days I resented it deeply. Rising before dawn throughout the summer to move irrigation pipes, putting down straw bedding for the cattle in the bitter cold of winter, seeing livestock die and having to dispose of the carcasses, removing heavy rocks from our fields, gathering and stacking an endless number of bales of hay while being attacked by mosquitoes, digging post holes by hand, being stuck on a tractor going round and around a field for hours—these are just some of the tasks that, by being annoying, frustrating, or exhausting, taught me that I didn't always want to belong. While city friends seemed to have the freedom to do with their days pretty much whatever they wanted, I was stuck within cycles of work that were unrelenting, often tedious, and regularly mocked by non-farm people. The very responsibilities that rooted me and told me where I belonged also sometimes felt like chains that confined, even humiliated, me.

Every fall one of our tasks was to haul cattle manure from the corrals out into the fields. The manure fed the soil that fed the plants that fed our cattle that fed us. Every summer you could see the line distinguishing fertilized from unfertilized land. The green of a manured field was more verdant, the stalks taller, and the heads of grain bigger. One evening, by the light of the moon, I was hauling the last load out for the day. Our equipment was old, and I didn't realize that the conveyer belt pushing the manure to the spreaders at the back of the wagon had somehow become engaged on my drive out. The more I drove, the more compacted the cow shit became. I knew I had a problem when the wheels on the wagon driving the belt locked. I couldn't move forward or head back.

I thought of abandoning the load and walking home, but that was a bad idea because by the next day the manure would have dried and hardened into a rock. I had no choice but to use my bare hands to claw at the cow shit. After about an hour of grueling effort, much of it punctuated by every curse word I knew, I managed to clear enough shit away for the wagon wheels to be operable. I could now count on the beaters to spread the rest. No matter how much I washed, the smell lingered on my body. I stunk of cow shit for days, as if I needed another reminder that farmwork could often be humiliating! I dreaded going to school.

But farmwork also afforded multiple pleasures. Attending the birth of a calf or a litter of piglets, breathing in the aroma of freshly cut hay, gathering eggs and shelling peas, watching grainfields turn from green to gold, listening to the munching of cattle eating fresh grass or rolled oats, seeing a well-constructed building put to good use, eating delicious food that I'd had a hand in producing—these all helped me feel that the work I did mattered and served a life-affirming end. The tedium was regularly interrupted by serendipitous encounters with a red-tailed hawk, a breathtaking sunrise or sunset, a muskrat ambling along in our marsh, the hilarious antics of piglets, the soothing smell and feel of a rain shower quenching a thirsty land, the honking of Canadian geese flying above in their enormous V-formations, the sighting of the occasional coyote or pronghorn antelope. These encounters reminded me of how magnificent and multifarious this world is. They put me in touch with realities that were profoundly other than me yet also amenable to my presence, even welcoming of it. Struggle, frustration, and inconvenience were common experiences. Nonetheless, I lived with a profound sense that my life fit here, even if the fit could be uncomfortable at times.

When I worked with sufficient attention, patience, and care, the farm taught me that this world isn't a massive warehouse or stockpile of natural resources waiting to be mined and commodified. It is a gracious and generative realm, a site of hospitality that is constantly making room and provision for life to thrive. I saw plenty of pain and suffering, but I also regularly saw life's will to flower and fruit. I knew that our land and its many creatures responded generously to a loving touch, and that healing was possible despite our mistaken efforts. The land's vitality and the depth and detail of its responsivity are why our world can be a place where hope grows.

Knowing that my labors were benefiting the many lives that made their home on our farm gave me a great deal of satisfaction. The work that rooted me could also make me feel—in the visceral modes of exertion and digestion—that my life, along with the lives of many other creatures, was quite literally growing out of the ground. Being in this place, I did not feel alone, abandoned, or worthless. I was stitched into a complex and dynamic fabric of being that included countless seen and unseen creatures and that enfolded more seasons of birth, germination, growth, illness, death, and decomposition than I could comprehend. My body didn't simply move on or across the land. It was a material expression of the sacred, mysterious, and sometimes terrifying powers of life that make this world beautiful, delicious, fragrant, melodious, and good. It was an expression of the powers of life precisely because it participated intimately and practically in them. The expansiveness of being, its generosity and grace, along with its inscrutability, were regularly on display.

Henry David Thoreau once suggested that we should think of our bodies as instruments through which the world sings. In a journal entry dated October 26, 1851, he said, "The instant I awoke, methought I was a musical instrument . . . My body was the organ and channel of melody, as a flute is of the music that is breathed through it. My flesh sounded and vibrated still to the strain, and my nerves were the chords of the lyre." But the enthusiasm of seeing himself as a listening and responding body was quickly dampened by "an infinite regret—to find myself, not the thoroughfare of glorious and world-stirring inspirations, but a scuttle full of dirt . . . my regret arose from the consciousness [of] how little like a musical instrument my body was now."[1]

The idea of the body as a musical instrument suggests that the best life is one that attunes itself to the places we are in and to the diverse creatures we are with. The best life is a *resonant* life that, like a tuning fork that responds to the vibration of another tuning fork, vibrates to the pulsing lives of others. Such a life is, as Thoreau suggested, like a flute that transforms breath into a melodious sound ranging from blues to jazz, from a plaintive cry to an exuberant dance. The key to a symphonic and harmonious life, which I take to be a life of deep belonging, is to develop the sympathy and affection that makes us want to be with others in ways that are courteous and mutually enhancing. To do so requires us to develop the improvisational skill that enables us to listen and accept, and that signals when we should stop, when we should move, and how. Much more than inclusion is at issue here, since a hopeful life depends on the knowledge that we are loved and nurtured and that we can be a source of nurture to others too.

Thoreau's oscillation between enthusiasm and regret signals what I take to be a fundamental challenge: to be in a place and be receptive to its power and potential. People, especially when living in contexts characterized by speed and mobility, can be oblivious to the generative grace and mystery of their surroundings. They can travel through a place without knowing how their living depends upon and grows out of it. Alternatively, people can be so rooted and attuned to where they are that they sense possibilities that, when realized, confirm that where they are is a good place to be. They have developed the patience and the practical skills that align and draw them more deeply into the pulses and rhythms of this life-sustaining world.

My maternal grandfather, Wilhelm Roepke, never read a word of Thoreau, but he understood Thoreau's sentiment and felt his longing. Working with him, I realized that here was a man who so loved our farm that he wanted to relish in and contribute to the manifold movements of its life. His was not a sentimental love: he knew the pain of injury, violation, and death (including the brutalities and horrors of World War II), and he endured the frustrations of thwarted plans, inclement weather, and recalcitrant livestock. What he understood from direct experience, however, was that he had not created his own life or the lives of the creatures that nurtured him. They were all a sacred gift, which is why he paused regularly to give thanks for the small blessings of each day. His manner with his animals was gentle and kind, his pacing unhurried. He did not take for granted the beauties or the fragilities of this life. He sought to honor the creatures under his care.

Let me give one example. We raised chickens, both the broilers we butchered to eat and the hens we kept to produce eggs. They had a coop of their own, but they were also free to move about the farmyard to look for grubs and bugs. From spring to fall my grandfather regularly paused after lunch, grabbed a bucket and a scythe, and cut some fresh grass to deliver to the chickens. This task became something of a ritual; the chickens knew what was coming. As Wilhelm walked toward them, they ran toward him in anticipation of the grass they were about to receive. As he threw the grass about, the chickens jumped and frolicked, gobbling whatever blades were closest to them. It was a moment of chicken joy, to be sure, but it also made my grandfather immensely happy.

Cutting and tossing around the grass was entirely unnecessary. The chickens had the run of the farm and could eat whatever grass they wanted. But he did it as an offering to them, to show that he cherished his chickens and believed that their happiness—not just their functioning—mattered. If the chickens were to nurture him at mealtimes, then he needed to nurture them in ways that respected and honored their chickenness. In facilitating their joy, he facilitated his own. I think of his small labor as a profound expression of the mutual nurture that is the beating heart of places of belonging and lives of hope.

One summer day our task was to go out into our freshly mowed hayfield and rake square corners at the ends of rows into round ones to make the hay easier to bale and to reduce waste. My grandfather and I quickly grew frustrated. The tines on the store-bought rakes were too short and too closely spaced together. We spent more time pulling tangled hay out of the rakes than we did putting it in rounded swaths. My grandfather suggested that we go back to the farmyard and make a better rake. Within an hour he had identified a poplar sapling, carved a handle, head, and several tines, and assembled the pieces to make a rake that was light, beautiful, and a pleasure to hold. We returned to the field where the superiority of this rake's design quickly became evident. Work that had been frustrating became easier and much more pleasurable.

I look back on this seemingly insignificant episode and see that my grandfather had developed the skills that enabled him to appreciate where he was, sense its possibilities, and turn his body into an instrument through which the farm's latent beauties could be realized and celebrated. As he saw it, to make something shoddy, disposable, or ugly was to insult the farm, which is why his rake needed to be both functional and beautiful. Every time I needed a rake, I sought out the one he made because it was a work of art and devotion and because it honored its user and the work to be done with it. In this rake the life of the poplar sapling vibrated, and the farm's energies—including the energy embodied in our labor—came together harmoniously.

The telling of this rake story wouldn't matter very much if it weren't that making and using the rake represented a whole manner of being that communicated a life of deep respect and belonging. My grandfather understood that he didn't simply live *on* a farm but *through* it and that in certain respects its diverse creatures, ranging from the earthworms in the soil to the dairy cow in the barn, created a home for him that was at once inspiring, nurturing, vexing, saddening, and beautiful. He knew the farm would take care of him if he learned to take care of it. Though he lived in the shadow of the Canadian Rockies and could remark on their beauty, he felt little need to visit them. The farm was where he wanted to be. I think he felt most fully alive when on his land and in the presence of his animals because he could feel their lives pulsating through his own. He could be in touch with the grace that sourced and sustained his world.

My aim is not to present my grandfather as a saint. He was often too suspicious of new machines and different ways of doing things, too dogmatic about some of his positions, and too accepting of the patriarchal sensibilities he had inherited (though he did later in life remark that husbands were not considerate enough of their wives and did not adequately honor the important work they did). My aim instead is to highlight his affection for the land and its creatures and to note that he represented the best of an agrarian way of being and belonging, a way of being that would soon be demolished by government policies and economic priorities that rewarded efficiency over affection, and short-term yield over long-term farm vitality.

My grandfather knew that his way of farming and his gentle and kind manner with animals were doomed. In his later years he saw that farming was being steered—mostly by corporate interests, global markets, and a demand for cheap food—into what has come to be called agribusiness. In the business of agriculture, neither land nor animals register as anything but commodities to be managed as efficiently and profitably as possible. The pressures of this system mean that farmers have great difficulty exercising the care and devotion they might otherwise like to practice. To be sure, this system is producing a lot of calories, more, in fact, than were ever produced in the history of agriculture. But the costs to farmers, farm communities, animals, soils, and waterways are immense when we take into account farmer indebtedness, depression, and suicide; the transformation of rural communities into ghettoes; the horrid conditions of farmworkers; the rates of soil erosion and degradation; the pollution and depletion of freshwater systems; the misery of billions of animals confined in inhumane conditions; and the unhealthiness of highly processed cheap food. This system depletes fertility, extinguishes diversity, compromises health, and eviscerates joy. It cannot be the basis of hope because it cannot inspire our love or devotion.

In *Braiding Sweetgrass* the botanist and Potawatomi citizen Robin Kimmerer says, "Knowing that you love the earth changes you, activates you to defend and protect and celebrate. But when you feel the earth loves you in return, that feeling transforms the relationship from a one-way street into a sacred bond."[2] So much in our world communicates the straining, even the severing, of the sacred bonds that join people to the earth and to each other. The straining of the bonds isn't any individual's fault; most people now find themselves living in urban centers and suburban neighborhoods where the bonds between people, the land itself, and all that the land provides are too difficult to maintain. The result is that people are deprived of the experience of knowing that the land loves them back. "I wonder," Kimmerer says, "if much that ails our society stems from the fact that we have allowed ourselves to be cut off from the love of, and from, the land. It is medicine for broken land and empty hearts."[3] Alone and unloved, people are severely damaged and hurt. They are likely to become anxious, arrogant, or destructive and to engage in behaviors, life-affirming or not, that aim to show others and themselves that they matter.

Kimmerer argues that we need to recover a "grammar of animacy," which is a way of perceiving, speaking, and engaging that honors the liveliness of places and the loveliness of creatures, a language that mirrors "the life that pulses through all things." In an animate world, no place or creature is a valueless object, some mere "it" that people can do with whatever they want. Instead, each is a valued member of a community of life that benefits and is benefited by the presence of every other member. Trees and streams and nuthatches are kin. Like family, they are vital members of the communities that nurture us. Our need of trees and streams and soils and butterflies is not optional. It is visceral and is witnessed every time we take a bite of food or a sip of water or a breath of fresh air. Our bodies thrive only because they move within and are nurtured by a world that is profoundly alive.

The remedy for a broken, lonely, and commodified world is fairly straightforward: nurture the places and creatures that nurture us. It is a simple remedy, but it is hardly an easy one, since relatively few people know what it takes to nurture others, especially plant and animal beings that are very different from themselves. Let's recall Thoreau's earlier lament that many of our sensory faculties are dull, which means that we don't really know (because we have not sufficiently practiced) the disciplines of patient and sustained listening, gentle and lingering touch, slow and savoring taste, fine and particularizing smell, and detailed and informed seeing that are the elements of good nurture. Nor do we possess the practical skills of attention, restraint, and care that make our presence a genuinely helpful presence. Given our dullness and lack of skill, Kimmerer advises planting a garden, even a small one. "It's good for the health of the earth and it's good for the health of people. A garden is a nursery for nurturing connection, the soil for cultivation of practical reverence . . . Something essential happens in a vegetable garden. It's a place where if you can't say 'I love you' out loud, you can say it in seeds. And the land will reciprocate, in beans."[4]

Sue Stuart-Smith agrees. In her book *The Well-Gardened Mind: The Restorative Power of Nature* she describes how gardens, even small urban ones, can be places of grounding, healing, and restoration. "Now, more than ever," she says, "we need to remind ourselves that first and foremost, we are creatures of the earth."[5] In times of grief, it is important to touch and smell and taste the goodness of the earth. In times of trouble, it is important to know that you can participate in activity that nurtures and re-creates the world. Gardening, however amateurishly or occasionally done, is important because it immerses people in the mysteries and flows of life that are at work in the soil and are constantly affecting the lives of flowers, fruits, vegetables, and trees. "When we sow a seed, we plant a narrative of future possibility. It is an action of hope."[6]

Stuart-Smith tells the story of Eddie, a war veteran suffering from PTSD. The war had damaged him profoundly. He felt ashamed and was deeply suspicious and frightened of others. Being in a group made him uneasy. He took to alcohol to dull the pain. It didn't take long for his family and his life to fall apart. But being in a garden slowly began to change him. The smell of a eucalyptus tree drew him in and damped down the toxic feelings he carried within. The sight of flowers rekindled the sense that he was part of something bigger than himself, something that is good and beautiful. As he began to work in the garden he came to understand that "everything is intertwined, everything has a purpose." He wasn't alone, nor was his life without value. Instead, communing with nature taught him to be amazed by life's beauties. "Wow! The color it just lifts you!"[7]

Trained as a psychiatrist and psychotherapist, Stuart-Smith realizes that there are limits to what gardens can accomplish. They are not an automatic cure for all that ails us. But what she learned by reading study after study and by visiting various garden projects was that people suffering from trauma and depression often found gardens to be places of refuge and affirmation. Others might judge and condemn them, but gardens accepted them. They discovered that they did not need to be perfect to plant a seed and see it grow. Enjoying a garden's fruit, they now knew that neither they nor their world was as bad as they had initially thought. Learning to take care of something as small as a row of lettuce or a flower patch was often enough to counteract the negative and self-destructive feelings that they had brought to the garden. In part, this is because the action of caring for another releases neurochemical rewards like oxytocin and beta-endorphins—the brain's natural opioids—which produce feelings of calm and contentment.

Being in a garden has the potential to change how people think about life. When people feel they have been abandoned or cast aside, or when they feel that life is worthless, gardens teach that life can be beautiful. When people feel disempowered or think that their life doesn't matter, tending a plant day after day gives them a sense of agency. When people perceive their world as a place of unremitting conflict and strife, gardening teaches them how to live with the environment rather than against it. It teaches them to feel good about themselves because they now see, smell, touch, and taste the goodness that is the fruit of their own efforts.

I am well aware that our future world will be overwhelmingly urban, which is why anything like a "back to the land" call is both naive and, for various reasons, ill advised. Even so, as many people as possible must be given regular and practical opportunities to get outside and stick their hands into the soil. Urban planners understand that green spaces play a crucial role in community well-being. They also know that today's urban poor suffer from debilitating mental and physical health conditions, living, as many of them do, in concrete spaces devoid of vegetation, fresh food, fragrant air, pleasing sights, and seasonal growth.

The proliferation of urban farms and gardens has been demonstrated to strengthen neighborhood communities. As people gather together to grow and share food, incidents of loneliness, vandalism, and antisocial behavior decrease. People report feeling more connected to one another and have a deepened sense of belonging to a neighborhood and a community. Studies have shown that garden projects are highly effective at promoting social integration. They become social and cultural centers, and by "providing a safe 'third space' outside home or work, they can help reduce community tensions. Their role in fostering community cohesiveness is particularly valuable in ethnically diverse neighborhoods, where this can otherwise be hard to achieve . . . Urban farms create a culture of collaboration, if not through shared produce, then shared pleasure."[8]

Gardens grow flowers and food. But by connecting people to soil, water, weather, plants, insects, animals, and fellow community members—the immediate and beneficial sources of our daily nurture—they also have the potential to grow hope.

5

A Forgiveness-Seeking Hope

As Don Ruzicka recalls it, the communication of forgiveness happened at roughly 6 a.m. on May 21, 2000. It came from an unlikely, what some might consider an impossible, source: a western meadowlark. Weighing in at 3–4 ounces and rarely longer than 10 inches, the lark isn't a big presence. But it is beautiful, with a yellow underside, a black V on its breast, and black dots striping its brown top. Don loved the sight of this bird and its watery, flutelike song, but he hadn't seen or heard one in over ten years.[1] That morning he was out in a pasture moving his chicken houses to fresh plots of grass when he heard a lark sing. Don stood at full attention and became completely still, wondering if his mind was playing tricks on him. Its second song sent him to the ground and on his knees. Its sound reverberated through his body and brought him to tears. In it he heard the land say, "I forgive you."

To understand the significance of this moment and Don's interpretation of the meadowlark's song, you need to know some of Don's story.[2]

Don's maternal grandparents moved to central Alberta in 1910, settling on land north and west of the town of Killam. Founded as a village in 1906, Killam sits on Treaty 6 land that was once home to fifty First Nations tribes, including Cree, Nakota, and Dene peoples.[3] Like so many European immigrants, Don's grandparents had moved west in pursuit of opportunity and a good life. They built a barn (in 1913) and then a house (in 1916). The farm prospered. Some of the family stayed on to do the work. When Don and Marie purchased the farm from Don's uncle and aunt in 1983, much of it was in pristine condition. They delighted in the knowledge that they were building on a family history and commitment to this particular piece of land. But as Don recalls, they were also excited to know that as owners they could now realize their dream.

During the 1980s, the push in agriculture from bankers, government officials, and agricultural experts was to industrialize production and maximize yield.[4] Across the Canadian West, wetlands and sloughs were drained, bush and woodlots cut down, and native prairie plowed up, all so that as many acres as possible could be planted in grain. Don was not immune to the pressures most farmers felt. He grew grain and raised as many cattle as he could for the commodities markets. Every year the pressure to increase yields in the face of dwindling profit margins mounted. To keep the farm going, loans to purchase ever-bigger machinery, hybrid seeds, fertilizers, and herbicides had to increase at the same time. An enormous debt load accrued. The stress went straight into Don's body. In March 1986 he was diagnosed with Crohn's disease.

Personal illness was not allowed to stand in the way of meeting ever-increasing production quotas. The work simply had to continue, even accelerate. It was exhausting and enormously stressful. By the fall of 1995, the year's grain harvest now completed, Don and Marie concluded that they had three options: (a) continue on this stressful journey of uncontrollable debt, (b) sell and move, or (c) try another way of farming. The first option didn't look very promising since continuing was, quite literally, destroying their lives and the fertility of the land. The second option was attractive because it represented a release from all the pressure. The third option was a bit unnerving. What would a different way of farming look like, and what would it require of them?

When Don went to town to pick up the mail the next day, an answer was waiting in the form of a one-page flyer inviting them to attend an information meeting to learn about Holistic Management. Don went to the meeting and discovered that Holistic Management is about farming in ways that restore land to health while also affording farmers and ranchers a sustainable way of life. Together, Don and Marie signed up for the eight-day course. In it they learned about ecosystem services, the value of riparian zones and native species, the dangers of pesticides and herbicides, and the importance of plant and animal species diversity. They also began to understand their complicity in farming practices that were systematically degrading and destroying the land. A crucial insight was dawning in their minds: as farmers, they do not simply live on the land but from it and through it as members of one vast community of life.

The following spring Don and Marie saw their farm with fresh eyes. They now understood that they were going to have to change their lives. The patterns of their daily work, the range of their affections and sympathies, the measurement of success and failure, and their idea of a good human life—all these needed to change if they were going to farm in ways that heal and nurture the land. Change was not going to be easy. They would need to unlearn twelve years of industrial methods and resist the pressure of banks and neighbors to continue in well-established and officially sanctioned ways. The risk they were taking was enormous. How would they pay their bills? Would they still be accepted by their community? The farm, a family history, and inherited ways of knowing, feeling, and working—all were on the line.

The following year, 1997, Don and Marie sold all their grain equipment and 320 acres of cultivated land. They converted the 600 remaining acres of cultivated land into pasture and planned to treat the 200 acres of native prairie, wetlands, and woods with newfound respect. A system of rotational grazing was put in place for the broilers, turkeys, laying hens, and hogs that were now a base of the farm operation. Cattle would be regularly moved through fenced-in paddocks in order not to overgraze pastureland or contaminate waterways flowing through their land. The goal going forward was to restore the land to vitality and health by giving it regular times to rest and replenish. By May 1999, Don and Marie had paid down all their debt. As Don puts it, "I am unable to clearly explain and do justice to how this removal of debt affected me. I felt as though I had been held hostage by the banking system, and now I was free!"

The freedom Don now felt was wholly unlike the freedom he had felt upon first purchasing the farm. In 1983 it was a freedom to do with the land whatever he wanted, a freedom to work out his dreams of personal and family success by making the land produce. In 1999 it was a freedom to serve the land and to nurture it to health, a freedom to give himself to the land (rather than to bankers) in work that facilitated multispecies flourishing.

To realize this new form of freedom, Don knew he was going to need a lot of help. It came in the form of teachers—biologists, riparian and agroforestry specialists, ornithologists, entomologists, ecologists, and range and wetland specialists—who gently and graciously offered their expertise. They helped him understand the damage that industrial methods had done to the land, and they showed him how to work with nature rather than against it. What followed was a complex, intensive management program that prioritized the protection of riparian zones, the replanting of roughly 100,000 trees, the reintroduction of native grasses and pollinator-friendly plants, and the creation of habitat for diverse wildlife species. As Don and Marie eliminated the use of poisons, repaired their water systems, and restored native grasses, flowers, bushes, and trees, they also created a hospitable habitat for microbes and insects, bees and butterflies, and birds and mammals to come back to. Along with the western meadowlark that sent Don to the ground, Swainson's hawks, Sprague's pipits, pileated woodpeckers, kingfishers, beavers, badgers, deer, and moose (to name just a few) returned to the farm. As Don understands it, their return is their confirmation of his efforts to repair and restore the land that he had damaged. In their return he feels the land's forgiveness and their willingness to live with him.

Don's experience of feeling forgiven by the land was preceded by his commitment to seek forgiveness. At first, Don would not have expressed his commitment or his work in exactly these terms, since little in his church or cultural formation spoke of the need to seek such forgiveness. How does a person go about asking for forgiveness from the land? Who, exactly, is being asked? Don didn't have clear answers to these questions. What he knew is that he needed to change his life and his ways of work if he wanted to live rightly on his farm. The years spent nurturing the land to health and restoring native species signaled his acknowledgment, what some might call his confession, that he had wronged the land and its creatures and that he needed to apologize for and repent of the practices that had damaged both. To seek forgiveness is to commit to naming, facing, and correcting the errors of past behaviors. It is to want to mend broken relationships and thus open the possibility of a better future life with others.

But as Don soon realized, a desire for forgiveness does not amount to a guarantee that forgiveness will be granted. Its granting cannot be forced. It takes the form of a gift. When Don spoke to visitors, he often gave them a tour of a 17-acre area that was once home to several sharp-tailed grouse nests. It was a lek, or breeding ground, where males danced each spring in a flurry of motion, tails pointed skyward, feet pounding the ground, with purple air sacs on each side of their throats inflated, all to attract females. In 1987 he had cleared the lek to grow more grain. Not a single grouse had been seen since, because once a lek is destroyed, grouse are highly unlikely to return. But Don did not give up. He describes his efforts to restore native grass and tree species as making "reparation for his sins." He says, "I may never create the habitat required for the sharp-tails to return, but hopefully other species will appear, and they have." Forgiveness is evolving, he says, as he does "the best I can to make things right with the land." He proposes a new organization, like "Ecological Sinners Anonymous," where people can tell their stories of mistakes made, but also of the repair work attempted, so that solutions for healing and right living can be shared with as many people as possible. The time is overdue, Don thinks, for citizens of industrial economies to engage in practices of confession and lament over the damage industrial methods are inflicting on lands and their communities of life.

I have told Don's story because I think hope depends on practices of confession, repentance, and forgiveness-seeking, practices that make it possible for people to live peaceably, perhaps even joyfully, with each other in the places of their shared life. I recognize that a story of forgiveness from the land is uncommon, since forgiveness is usually a practice that happens between people. To restrict the scope of forgiveness to interpersonal relationships, however, is a mistake, because the harms people do and have done are not confined to other people. They extend to the land and to nonhuman creatures. We live in a deeply damaged and wounded world where most ecosystems, along with many of our urban neighborhoods, bear the marks of humanity's pillaging, poisoning, and profiteering ways. Of course, not all people share the same responsibility for the damage done; some have been far more negligent or destructive than others. Even so, the prospect of a future of mutual flourishing depends on people working to name the wrongs that have been or are being done—which includes learning how the wrongs came about by listening carefully and nondefensively to those voicing the harm—and then committing to work with those harmed to repair the damage. Hoping for a healthy humanity doesn't make sense if our homes, neighborhoods, fields, watersheds, and forests are sick and dying.

In *The Book of Forgiving,* Archbishop Desmond Tutu and his daughter Mpho say that when people seek forgiveness, they signal their desire to create paths of healing on which people can walk and work together again. They seek to mend the brokenness and alienation caused by envy, fear, anger, loneliness, and arrogance because they appreciate that the best life is one in which people come alongside each other in postures of care, humility, and respect. Their crucial insight is that forgiveness opens the door to healing. With forgiveness, people can experience and realize their full humanity. "When we have done wrong and seek to make it right, we show the depth of our humanity. We reveal the depth of our desire to heal ourselves. We show the depth of desire to heal those we have harmed."[5] People cannot live in hopeful ways if the relationships that should inspire, nourish, and fulfill their living are broken.

If we are honest with ourselves, we see that a need to seek

forgiveness is a permanent condition. I do not believe that people are inherently or continuously malicious. But they do regularly make mistakes, choose inappropriately, think confusedly, and behave in ways that are either negligent, blind, arrogant, or mean—sometimes without intending to do any of these things. To seek forgiveness is not to ask for a magic wand that erases or undoes the damage done in the past. In many cases, the wounds remain as a (potentially instructive) reminder of the harms done. Seeking forgiveness starts, instead, with the admission that we have wronged others and now want to make things right or at least better. As Matthew Ichihashi Potts has rightly observed, "Forgiveness seeks to live in the wake of loss. It accepts that what has been lost cannot be restored, and then it aims to live in and with the irrevocability of wrong."[6]

Admitting a wrong done, saying "I am sorry," doesn't come easily. The temptation is to become defensive. The trouble with a self-justifying posture, however, is that it leaves people cut off from those they have harmed. In cases like this, we need the help of others to name the wrongs we cannot ourselves see, and then we need to have them come alongside as we figure out what a better way looks like and entails. We need them to say that they will not abandon us despite our wrongdoing. "When we are willing to let down our defences and look honestly at our actions, we find there is a great freedom in asking for forgiveness and great strength in admitting the wrong. It is how we free ourselves from our past errors. It is how we are able to move forward into our future, unfettered by the mistakes we have made."[7] Guilt and shame are crushing burdens to live with. They keep us mired in the past and often keep us lonely.

Desmond and Mpho Tutu believe that when people harm someone, they harm themselves at the same time. To live well and to achieve the most that life offers, people need the help of each other. Life is a deeply communal reality. No creature can flourish alone. To thrive we must constantly receive from and give to others various forms of inspiration, nurture, instruction, and friendship. We are needy beings from the womb to the tomb. This neediness is why it is so important to identify when and where we have harmed the relationships that sustain us, show genuine remorse for the harm done, and then commit to being a healing presence going forward. The search for forgiveness is not a selfish gesture, even as it clearly benefits our own lives. It is, instead, a form of accountability in which people signal their willingness to live in ways that honor and respect those they depend upon. "By asking for forgiveness, we are committing ourselves to the possibility of change. We are signing up for the hard work of transformation."[8]

Transformation is not reconciliation, especially if by reconciliation we mean something like the forgetting of past wrongs, the concealing of wounds, or the assumption of an easy harmony. Wounds often remain as the visible reminder that the trauma is having ongoing effects that require correction, patience, forbearance, and mercy. In cases of continuing trauma, asking the wronged person to live amicably with the wrongdoer cures nothing and may even be cruel. What the person in pain requires is a community of support that provides a protective space in which processes of healing might occur.

Let me put it another way. When people lament histories of wrongdoing and commit to being a helping and healing presence going forward, they also begin to shed the self-justifying strategies that keep them from being in a respectful relationship with the wounded. They shed the illusion that they themselves are innocent and exempt from a need to change. Confession and repentance signal the commitment to name and be instructed by the pain and suffering of the past, all so that people can work together for a better future. A desire for forgiveness plays the important role of making it possible for people in the present to have an honest and educative relationship with the past. The granting of forgiveness, in turn, liberates people into a future, because they now know that even in the face of error and wrongdoing, they can begin again. *Now* they can partner with others, including those wronged, in the healing of a wounded world.

Don's story helps us see that relationships that support human flourishing must include the land and all its creatures. If those relationships are broken, human flourishing is subverted and frustrated. Why? Because there is no healthy or vibrant human life apart from fertile soil, clean water, fresh air, healthy microbiomes, copious insects and pollinators, and a profusion of diverse plant and animal life. Every breath, swallow, and gulp we make is a daily confirmation of that fact. The implications that follow from this insight are enormous. The most profound is the recognition that we may have greatly misjudged what we understand a person to be. People are not single, solitary, self-standing, self-sourcing beings. They are so intricately and intimately stitched into vast and complex webs of mutuality with creatures large and small, and within a bewildering array of geo-eco-bio-chemical processes, that the idea of a neatly circumscribed human identity breaks down. To be human is to be fully immersed with and dependent upon creatures that are not human. To live as fully as possible requires that we live mercifully and peaceably with all the creatures that are not us.

In my conversations with Don, he said that his commitment to heal his land and welcome plant and animal creatures back went hand in hand with a growing appreciation for the land and its creatures as kin. Over time, and with much newfound attention and effort, Don came into the presence of what he calls "the spirit of the land," the felt sense that the land isn't simply a piece of private property but a community with integrity and sanctity. It has a life of its own that calls forth wonder and respect. It can be harmed and violated, and it has a moral, even personal, claim upon his life. The land does not simply belong to him. He also belongs to it, and is accepted by it, as one who grows out of the ground and is nurtured by its life. The goal is to be in resonant relationship with it.

Over time Don was learning to see himself as but one member of a community of life that included countless creatures and was characterized by mutual need and help. He came to the realization that his happiness and success were inextricably bound up with the health and vitality of his farm. To know the needs of his land and to offer his help became a sacred calling that affirmed the goodness and beauty of his world. Insofar as Don was committed, like fellow farmers, to "making the land pay," the land was mute and reduced to a commodifiable object that had lost any spiritual or moral resonance. But as Don learned to sense his need of others and then appreciated, even embraced, that need, he also came to realize how precious life together is. The hope that Don now feels is not the result of what he has done. Instead, hope has grown in him as he has learned to make his love—his attention, energy, and skill—a participation in what he believes to be the sacred power that creates and sustains the land and its many creatures.

Don is well aware that his search for forgiveness is not complete. In part, this is because he is caught within processes and systems that he does not fully comprehend or control. What, for instance, is he to do with the fact that his farm sits on Treaty 6 land, land that formerly and since time immemorial belonged to First Nations tribes? Don did not himself displace Indigenous peoples, even though he has been the beneficiary of histories and policies that did. The larger question is, what responsibilities do whole communities, institutions, and governments have to the many Indigenous peoples who have been forcibly removed from their lands, oppressed, and killed in the name of progress and development?

On July 25, 2022, in Maskwacis, Alberta, a community not far from Don's farm, Pope Francis delivered a formal apology to First Nations peoples. He came in response to an invitation from Indigenous leaders who had traveled to the Vatican to meet with Francis four months earlier. At that time one elder presented Francis with a pair of children's moccasins, asking that he return them to her community when he came to Alberta to apologize and listen. Calling his journey to Alberta a "penitential pilgrimage," Francis said, "I have come to your native lands to tell you in person of my sorrow, to implore God's forgiveness, healing and reconciliation, to express my closeness and to pray with you and for you." He said unambiguously: "I humbly beg forgiveness for the evil committed by so many Christians against the Indigenous Peoples."[9]

Christian churches have much to be sorrowful about and seek forgiveness for: the forced removal of Indigenous children from their families and their placement in residential schools where they suffered physical, verbal, psychological, sexual, and spiritual abuse (between 1880 and 1990 roughly 150,000 children were placed in just over 130 Canadian schools, with over half of these run by the Roman Catholic Church); the marginalization and suppression of Indigenous languages and ways of life; the continuing intergenerational trauma that is the result of broken communities and traditions; and the deaths of countless Indigenous peoples owing to starvation, disease, neglect, rape, and murder.

During the visit, Francis stressed the importance of not forgetting the pain and suffering that representatives of the church had caused. He noted that the land itself speaks to us and "preserves the scars of still open wounds" (the discovery of unmarked graves in school cemeteries showed rampant disease, abuse, and death by suicide). It is important, he said, for people to "make space for memory." Learning about the past and grieving together are important first steps on the path toward forgiveness, because when people forget a painful past, they also become indifferent to the afterlives of that pain as it is being felt in the present. "We want to walk together, to pray together and work together, so that the sufferings of the past can lead to a future of justice, healing and reconciliation."[10]

To walk and work with others presupposes a willingness to be taught and corrected by them. As Francis made clear in his encyclical *Laudato Si': On Care for Our Common Home,* the colonial expansion of Europe rested upon forms of "development" that were disrespectful of Indigenous practices and ways of knowing, and destructive of Indigenous homes and lands. Colonists walked over and pushed aside the Indigenous people they encountered. Speaking there in Maskwacis, he apologized for this colonial history. Whereas colonists have done much damage to places and people, Indigenous peoples have long respected the land and worked to preserve it for future generations. "You have treated it as a gift of the Creator to be shared with others and to be cherished in harmony with all that exists, in profound fellowship with all living beings." Whereas Western cultures were forming people who were caught in the grip of selfishness and acquisitiveness, Indigenous peoples were holding a "treasury of sound customs and teachings, centered on concern for others, truthfulness, courage and respect, humility, honesty and practical wisdom." Francis made the point that a hopeful future—that is, a future in which the remembered past can serve to inspire and inform better ways of being together, and thereby become a future that people want to commit themselves to—depends on mutual correction and respect.

But asking for forgiveness is only a first step. Francis acknowledged that the essential work is now to create a culture able to prevent past horrors from happening again. Efforts must be made to repair the damage that has been done, even though these efforts will never accomplish enough. Drawing upon his own Christian tradition, Francis appealed to the loving way of life of Jesus, who, in his ministries of feeding, healing, and friendship, showed what it takes, practically speaking, to come alongside others in ways that promote their flourishing. He directed attention to Jesus's grave, "which seemed the burial place of every hope and dream, leaving behind only sorrow, pain and resignation," and noted that his resurrection from the dead holds the promise of a new beginning and new life animated by love and directed to universal reconciliation.

Moving forward, the crucial test will be whether Francis's plea for forgiveness stays at the level of a formal pronouncement or becomes realized in specific policies and structures that practically benefit the Indigenous communities that have been harmed. Indigenous leaders are watching closely to see whether the church is truly repentant and is thus prepared to reject former teachings like the "Doctrine of Discovery." Drawn out of fifteenth-century papal bulls, it was used to justify the colonization of non-Christian lands.[11] Indigenous leaders are waiting to see whether the church provides the economic assistance they need to address mental and physical health concerns, along with housing and educational needs. They are waiting to see if the church can be trusted as a partner committed to working for their good. Too many of the promises made to Indigenous peoples by government and religious leaders, beginning with the treaties that took away their ancestral lands in exchange for vital services, have been broken. For Indigenous peoples to live in hope, they need to know that their lands will be restored and that their ways of life are respected. The search for forgiveness must at the same time be a search for reconciliation, healing, and repair.[12]

There is no single, universally applicable blueprint for the work of reconciliation. The details of redress, repair, and reparation will be unique to each context as parties come together over the particular histories that they share. Moreover, the work of reconciliation takes time, for people must come into each other's presence, genuinely listen, and develop a mutual sympathy.

To see what is at stake and what is possible, consider the story of Art and Helen Tanderup, both farmers in Nebraska. Their farm has been in Helen's family since the late nineteenth century, but it sits on land that belonged to the Ponca tribe. Like so many other Indigenous groups around the world, Ponca people were forcibly evicted from their homes and marched to a reservation far away (despite being on peaceable and friendly terms with white settlers in the area where they lived). Along the 600-mile journey to Oklahoma, several of the tribe's members died. When the Poncas arrived at the reservation, they discovered that the government had made no provision for them. They also arrived too late to plant food crops. In the ensuing months roughly one quarter of them died from hunger and disease.

The Tanderups did not know any of this history when they took over the farm. They only learned of it because, along with members of the Poncas tribe, they opposed the construction of the Keystone XL Pipeline, which threatened to poison the groundwater that made up the Ogallala Aquifer. While the Tanderups and the Poncas protested together, they moved from being political allies to being personal friends. The Tanderups hosted a "spirit camp" where area farmers and tribal members spent several winter days together. A tepee was raised, fires were kept, and stories were shared. This is how the Tanderups came to know the Poncas' painful history. They learned of the widespread theft of Indigenous lands and the many crimes (assault, rape, neglect) against Indigenous peoples. The camp is also where the Tanderups and the Poncas decided to form an uncommon alliance centered on the planting of corn.

The Poncas tribe had grown corn for generations on what was now the Tanderups' land. A Poncas elder by the name of Mekasi Horenik asked if they might again plant their sacred corn on their ancestral lands. Art and Helen eagerly embraced the idea and made an acre of land available for their use. But would the sacred corn grow? The specific varieties of corn that Mekasi had in mind were kept in a medicine bundle and had not been planted in over a hundred years. When the seeds germinated, the Tanderups and the Poncas people were elated.

In subsequent years, members of the Poncas tribe came in the spring to plant and in the fall to harvest. But the fifth year was going to be special. That spring a ceremony was held on the farm in which Art and Helen signed a new "treaty" that returned what was eventually to become 10 acres of land to tribal members. At the ceremony Art said the treaty was many years in the making. The possibility was born while Tanderups and Poncas were sitting together in a tepee talking and listening to each other's stories. "We talked about bringing the corn back to its homeland. We talked about the homeland being taken away from the people. We talked about growing that corn again. And making all the relatives healthy." Art knows that their gesture is small, a very modest gesture aiming to make amends for a painful history of dispossession and abuse. "So this is a small gesture . . . It can never make what went wrong right, but it can show how we feel about this and how we are honored to give this small piece of land back to the people that . . . were the stewards of this land. They took care of it. They knew how to take care of it." Upon the signing of the treaty, Casey Camp-Horinek, a councilwoman of the southern Poncas tribe and Mekasi's mother, was overcome with emotion. She said, "This day our Mother the Earth sustained us, and gave us reason to live. This day the wind is blessing us . . . allowing us to become one spirit."[13]

6

A Forgiveness-Granting Hope

On March 3, 1986, Christopher Piet, along with six members of the anti-apartheid group known as the Gugulethu Seven, was shot and killed by officers of the South African police. Ranging in age from sixteen to twenty-three, these seven young men had become the focus of a government-sponsored death squad, based in the secret camp Vlakplaas, that was tasked with securing South Africa's apartheid regime. In the weeks leading up to the attack, Vlakplaas operatives infiltrated Piet's group, gained their trust, and trained them for military combat. The assignment given to the seven young men was to attack a bus carrying senior police officers making its way into Gugulethu station. But it was a trap. Twenty-five well-armed police were waiting for them at the station with grenades and assault rifles. In the ensuing bloodbath Christopher and his six friends were murdered.

Ten years later, on April 23, 1996, Piet's mother, Cynthia Ngewu, spoke before South Africa's Truth and Reconciliation Commission (TRC). She said that on the day of the attack she had gone to the police station after learning that several young people had been shot. She feared that her son might be among them. Police officers informed her that they did not keep a list of the killed. They told her to go to the mortuary. Though her son had been shot in the head twelve times, it didn't take long for her to identify his body. She discovered what had happened to him by watching the evening news on television. "I saw my child," she said. "I actually saw them dragging him, there was a rope around his waist, they were dragging him with the van." The postmortem found twenty-five bullet wounds.

Ngewu says that at the time she was full of hatred for white people. Having seen the brutal manner in which her son was killed, she didn't want to see another white man. She thought they were without feeling, that they had lost their humanity. But during the TRC hearing she said, "We do not want to return evil by another evil. We simply want to ensure that the perpetrators are returned to humanity." She wanted everyone to embrace the idea of a reconciled society. When asked if she wanted to see the perpetrators punished, she said: "We do not want to see people suffer in the same way that we did suffer . . . We would like to see peace in this country . . . I think that all South Africans should be committed to the idea of re-accepting these people back into the community. We do not want to return the evil that perpetrators committed to the nation. We want to demonstrate humaneness toward them, so that they in turn may restore their own humanity."[1]

Ngewu was not alone in expressing a desire for reconciliation with her offenders. Pearl Faku and Doreen Mgoduka became widows in 1989 when the police car their husbands were driving exploded. The explosion wasn't an accident. White police officers who wanted to silence these Black officers had planted the bomb because the Black officers were threatening to expose their involvement in the killing of four Black anti-apartheid activists. The order to bomb the car came from the commander of the police, Nic van Rensberg, but the plan was devised by Eugene de Kock. De Kock instructed the technicians at the Pretoria police department to build a remote-controlled bomb. In case anything went wrong he developed a contingency plan to have the Black police officers executed by agents recruited from Vlakplaas. The contingency plan proved to be unnecessary. The bomb exploded as planned, killing Faku's and Mgoduka's husbands, along with two other men.

As de Kock concluded his testimony before the TRC in 1997, he asked if he could meet with the widows. He wanted to apologize. Their lawyer agreed to the meeting. A few days later Faku and Mgoduka were interviewed by Pumla Gobodo-Madikizela, a clinical psychologist who served on the Human Rights Violation Committee of the TRC. Faku said in the interview that she was profoundly touched by de Kock's acknowledgment of their pain and by the sorrow he felt for having caused it. She broke into tears. "I couldn't control my tears. I could hear him, but I was overwhelmed by emotion, and I was just nodding, as a way of saying yes, I forgive you. I hope that when he sees our tears, he knows that they are not only tears for our husbands, but tears for him as well . . . I would like to hold him by the hand, and show him there is a future, and that he can still change."[2]

The forgiveness-granting gestures of these women, along with the empathy, kindness, and mercy they demonstrated, are remarkable, especially when we recall that from the inception of South Africa in 1910, Black people were systematically excluded from participation in political life. Politicians at the time thought equality between Blacks and whites "an absurdity." Though apartheid did not become a formal policy until 1948, proclamations about Black inferiority had been made for years. White leadership maintained that the future of South Africa depended on racial purity, hence the need to keep Blacks and whites "apart." Policies were put in place that legalized and violently enforced discrimination at all levels. Blacks were forcibly removed from their lands (which were then given to whites) and had their homes demolished. They were systematically excluded from jobs that were reserved for white people. Black people were told that their lot in life was to be a source of cheap labor for agriculture and industry. They were consigned to inferior, all-Black schools that were designed to relegate Blacks to positions of perpetual servitude. They were denied the right to vote. Their protests against government policies were ruthlessly suppressed. Whites and Blacks were not permitted to intermingle in public, and intermarriage was strictly forbidden. The minister of native affairs, Dr. H. F. Verwoerd, argued for a state apparatus in which any hope of racial equality was systematically denied and any hope that Blacks might have for a free and prosperous life was systematically frustrated. Nelson Mandela, in 1955, shortly before his first arrest, said, "The spectre of Belsen and Buchenwald is haunting South Africa."[3]

The African National Congress (ANC) was formed in 1912 to advocate for racial equality. For decades members campaigned on the idea that South Africa belonged to whites *and* Blacks. Their protests were nonviolent. On March 21, 1960, however, police opened gunfire on hundreds of Black people who had gathered in Sharpeville to march and protest the "pass laws" that restricted the movement of Blacks. Sixty-nine were killed, and 186 were wounded, many of them women and children, many of them shot in the back while fleeing. The Sharpeville Massacre ignited protests across the country. The government responded with "emergency" measures that banned anti-apartheid activity and gave its police force free reign to use whatever violence necessary to enforce apartheid policies. A reign of state-sanctioned terror followed.

The ANC now recognized that force needed to be met with counterforce. The government's security forces and murder squads relied on informers to identify anti-apartheid activists.

Thousands of suspects were detained without trial. Many died under torture while in detention, and hundreds more were murdered by apartheid's death squads. As prime minister, P. W. Botha launched a "Total Strategy" for deploying any means necessary to preserve white supremacist policies. Torture, kidnapping, disappearances, mysterious deaths, and mass killings became commonplace. Police were given immense power and complete immunity from prosecution. Their aim was to eliminate every threat to apartheid.

Mandela was foremost among these threats. Mandela had joined the ANC in 1942, and soon thereafter (1947) became the elected secretary of the African National Congress Youth League. Trained as a lawyer, Mandela was an astute and articulate leader, becoming the Youth League's president in 1952. When the ANC was banned in 1960, Mandela went underground, but he continued his organizing work. In 1962 he was betrayed by an informer, arrested, and sent to prison. In 1963, while still in prison, Mandela was back in court again, this time under charges of sabotage and conspiracy to overthrow the government. His sentence was life imprisonment on Robben Island. Being in prison didn't halt his efforts. Throughout his time there, he remained committed to the Freedom Charter of the ANC, which stated that South Africa belonged to Blacks and whites alike. He told his captors, "We do not want to drive you into the sea."[4]

Upon his release from prison on February 11, 1990, Mandela reiterated his commitment to the ANC. Even though the movement's armed struggle never added up to much, he had declined to call a halt to it from prison, declaring that only free individuals could negotiate. But he also wanted to be clear that violence could not create or sustain a lasting peace. Genuine peace could not be built on the hatred of whites. "I knew that people expected me to harbor anger towards whites. But I had none. In prison, my anger towards whites decreased, but my hatred for the system grew. I wanted South Africa to see that I loved even my enemies while I hated the system that turned us against one another." He told reporters that South Africa's future depended on white inclusion and participation. "We did not want to destroy the country before we freed it, and to drive the whites away would devastate the nation."[5]

Mandela's commitment to an inclusive politics was regularly tested. South Africa's president, F. W. de Klerk, had made a few promising gestures to roll back some of apartheid's policies, but as the date of a national election drew closer—the first in which Blacks would vote—there was an upsurge in violence and police oppression. Ten days before the election, Mandela and de Klerk participated in their sole televised election debate. Both parties were suspicious and highly critical of each other, with Mandela accusing the National Party of fanning race hatred and division, and de Klerk claiming that the ANC did not know how to rule responsibly. As the debate drew to a close, Mandela felt that he had been too harsh. He said that their disagreements should not be allowed to obscure their common loyalty and love for their shared country. If he was elected, he said, he would rely upon de Klerk to help solve the problems South Africans faced. After making this point, he reached over to take de Klerk's hand, saying, "I am proud to hold your hand for us to go forward."[6]

How should we understand Pearl Faku's desire to hold the hand of de Kock, the man widely considered to be the most brutal of apartheid police assassins, and Mandela's desire to take the hand of de Klerk, the leader of the political party responsible for immeasurable suffering? Should anyone want to welcome and work together with former killers in building a better future? What are the implications—for perpetrators and victims—of refusing to accept an apology? If they refuse, do they thereby close the door to personal transformation? Do people excuse too much brutality and violation if they grant forgiveness? Do they make light of the pain and injustice victims suffer?

The white poet and writer Antjie Krog, reflecting on her years-long reporting on the Truth and Reconciliation Commission proceedings, said she was wholly unprepared for the mercy and the magnanimity with which victims often responded to the people who had violated them. "I felt how the whole framework within which I had been raised was limping, deaf and dumb." Listening to Black people testify, many of them poor and maimed, many of them women, she was struck by the fact that so many refused retaliation and revenge. They often wanted contact, contrition, and compassion instead. They expressed their desire for a future in which Blacks and whites could live together in peace.

In Krog's estimation, the hearings set a new foundation and trajectory for South Africa and for the world, a new basis for understanding and navigating life with others that seemed both superior to what she knew and necessary for the years ahead. If at one time Krog had firmly adhered to an individualistic ethic and a self-reliant ethos, she now realized that the way forward in South Africa needed to be based on inclusion and belonging and needed to proceed with an "ubuntu" understanding that says, "a person is made into being a person by other persons" and that people need each other to be whole.[7] The often-expressed desire that perpetrators be "returned to their humanity" is based on the assumption that people are not individuals responsible for making it on their own but are members of communities that can help them repent and heal. The aim of having many victims testify was not to humiliate and demonize perpetrators, and thereby exclude them from social life, but to find ways to restore perpetrators to their best selves so they could be contributing members in their communities and committed to mutual flourishing. Among the many tragedies that Krog identified as having defined South Africa, racism, colonialism, and apartheid were foremost because they eroded the ubuntu values and practices of communality that she now saw as essential to South Africa's healing.[8]

Archbishop Desmond Tutu, in his own reflections as chair of the TRC, also spoke of the crucial significance of ubuntu teaching for the work of reconciliation. To live an ubuntu way of life is to affirm that one's own humanity is intimately and inextricably bound up with the humanity of others. To degrade another is to degrade oneself. To nurture another is to nurture oneself. This mutual responsiveness is why it is so important that people practice generosity, hospitality, friendliness, forbearance, and compassion with each other. When these practices are in force, everyone benefits. But when others are hurt or humiliated, the whole community suffers. Conflict, violence, and resentment undermine the ability of a community and each person in it to maximally realize their potential. There can be no genuine freedom for any one person so long as other people are still in chains.[9]

As Tutu led the TRC proceedings he became more and more convinced that there was no hope for South Africa—in fact, no hope for our brutalizing and violent world—apart from forgiveness. Without forgiveness, individuals and communities remain locked in cycles of resentment, blame, retaliation, and revenge, all of which keep people estranged, alone, or at war with each other. Tutu was clear that forgiveness was not about excusing the injustices done or minimizing the harms felt. It was about believing in the possibility of a better future and then committing to the practical steps that would move people there. "In the act of forgiveness we are declaring our faith in the future of a relationship and in the capacity of the wrongdoer to make a new beginning on a course that will be different from the one that caused the wrong . . . It is an act of faith that the wrongdoer can change."[10] To refuse to forgive is to create more victims, to create more people debilitated by guilt, rage, hate, or vengeance. To grant forgiveness is to open paths for mutual understanding and healing, paths where people can come into each other's presence, be transformed, and (potentially) learn to care for each other.

Victims testifying at the TRC hearings displayed tremendous courage in telling their stories and confronting the people who had hurt them. On the one hand, they showed that they were able to take charge of their own destinies and were not going to allow those who had injured them to confine them to a state of perpetual victimhood.[11] On the other hand, they risked being disbelieved and having their shame amplified. But they also showed tremendous sympathy for those who had violated them. They understood that members of the South African police, for instance, were also victims of brutalizing behaviors that dehumanized them, behaviors sanctioned (and rewarded) by state and society. Those testifying understood that many of the people who behaved violently had grown up in abusive and negligent households and in communities that had failed them.

The courage and sympathy these women expressed was not without profound sadness and sometimes incapacitating anger. The offer of forgiveness was occasionally a pragmatic step to find a way to move forward in contexts of unspeakable grief and personal bewilderment. In other words, the offer of forgiveness was not guaranteed. In many instances, it could not even be expected, because the people at the table were so racked by personal pain. People coming to the table did not know what effects their words would have or whether they would be able to speak the same words on another day.

Gobodo-Madikizela recalls the meeting in which the officer responsible for luring the Gugulethu Seven to their deaths met with their mothers. The mothers were very angry with him and accused him of being a wolf dressed in sheep's clothing. The man was shaking and twitching in his chair. When he looked the mothers in the face, he referred to them as "my parents" and asked for forgiveness "from the bottom of my heart." There was silence. Then Cynthia Ngewu said to the man that he was the same age as her son Christopher Piet. "I want to tell you, my son, that I, as Christopher's mother, I forgive you, my son. I want you to go home knowing that I have forgiven you. Yes, I forgive you: I am at peace. Go well, my son." As the man prepared to leave the room, several of the other mothers embraced him.[12]

Among the mothers who offered their forgiveness, several used the word *inimba* to describe how they felt. *Inimba* translates as "umbilical cord" and thereby communicates maternal and bodily empathy. "To feel *inimba* is to feel like a mother does for a child when her child is in pain." What shocked Gobodo-Madikizela is that these women responded to the murderers as if they were their own sons. "As they would forgive their own child, they forgive this man; they assume responsibility for him and, in so doing, bring him back into the communal fold where his humanity might be restored."[13] Would they have said this to a white male perpetrator? Would a Black male victim have spoken the way these women did?

Gobodo-Madikizela recognizes that it is dangerous to essentialize a woman's womb and to expect women to carry the burden of a society to forgive offenders. Even so, she wonders if the embodied attachment and visceral sympathy that an umbilical cord communicates says something profound about the depth of our need of and responsibility for each other. Does maternal experience yield a crucial insight about the kind of empathy people need to learn to effect genuine healing and reconciliation? The use of the word *inimba* in these contexts indicates that ubuntu is not simply an idea or even an emotion but a form of responsibility and an ethical force that is felt and realized *through the body*. Perhaps we should think of these women as teaching the world that men and women need to behave like a maternal body that protects and nurtures others whether they have given biological birth to them or not.[14]

The Tutus believe that "the ability to forgive others comes from the recognition that we are all flawed and all human. We all have made mistakes and have harmed others. We will again."[15] They are not suggesting that all offenses are the same or that the choices people make to forgive are made from a position of personal confidence or cognitive clarity. Instead, they are noting that it is dangerous to assume that any of us are in complete control over our own virtue or vice. The logic of ubuntu cuts both ways. Communality inspired by solicitude, humility, and compassion can be the practical context that best forms people to behave decently and honorably. But when shared life comes to be animated by suspicion, jealousy, fear, or hatred, it can also be the matrix that degrades or destroys the best capacities latent within each one of us.

How do we develop sympathy for another, especially when that other has behaved violently? Gobodo-Madikizela explored this question in a particularly insightful manner in her encounters with de Kock, the mastermind behind so much Black suffering and the widely acknowledged embodiment of apartheid evil. During one of their interviews, de Kock wept upon recalling his encounter with Faku and Mgoduka. He said he wanted to have done more than say he was sorry for murdering their husbands: "I wish I could say, 'Here are your husbands,' he said, stretching out his arms as if bearing an invisible body, his hands trembling, his mouth quivering, 'but unfortunately . . . I have to live with it.'" Upon witnessing him weeping, Gobodo-Madikizela reached out and touched his shaking hand. It was rigid, cold, and clenched (he later told her it was his trigger hand). Her sympathetic reaction surprised her. She quickly withdrew her hand. Remembering who she was touching, she recoiled and rethought her spontaneous act of reaching out as "something incompatible with the circumstances of an encounter with a person who not too long ago had used these same hands, this same voice, to authorize and initiate unspeakable acts of malice against people very much like myself."[16]

A range of emotions flooded Gobodo-Madikizela's mind as she drove home from this meeting. Was her reaching out a display of compassion or perhaps some identification with his humanity? Did she feel sorry for de Kock, sensing in his vulnerability and sadness a glimmer of the decent man he might have become had that side of him not been buried under apartheid's brutality? Was he trying to assert his power over her or seeking to elicit unwarranted sympathy? She felt anger at the system that first created and now presumed to condemn him. She wondered whether he wanted the touch as some reassurance that he, or at least some part of him, was worthy of being touched. The memory of touching him also caused her to realize a truth she did not want to acknowledge—namely "that good and evil exist in our lives, and that evil, like good, is always a possibility. And that was what frightened me."[17]

Some colleagues believed that Gobodo-Madikizela was being manipulated by de Kock. They publicly told her so at a meeting of psychoanalysts from North America, the United Kingdom, and South Africa. Albie Sachs, a judge on South Africa's Constitutional Court and himself a victim of a bomb attack, came to her defense. He stressed how important it is to see the humanity of the perpetrators of violence. He stressed that unless people reach out in a spirit of compassion to wrongdoers, the cycles of retaliation and revenge will continue. Hope resides in the belief that wrongdoers can, despite their wrongdoing, be affirmed as fundamentally good and capable of change. Wrongdoers need to feel that they can be welcomed back into the community of humanity. They need to know that they have not been abandoned or dismissed as moral monsters beyond the pale of redemption. Of course, they also need to know that readmission into the community requires of them the hard work of making amends and striving for peace. To do that work, however, requires that they (with the help of others) discover the goodness that is deep within themselves and cultivate it in the world. To denounce others as monsters is doubly morally problematic because it places them outside the possibility of behaving better and because it excuses communities from having to accept any responsibility for how their lives turned out. To deny the abiding goodness of people, and to deny the possibility of their transformation in a community, is to forfeit the possibility of a hopeful life.[18]

Tutu, Krog, Gobodo-Madikizela, and others working with the TRC understood that the work of forgiveness is ongoing. It doesn't end when a perpetrator confesses and offers an apology, or when a victim says, "I forgive you." A genuine apology "must communicate, convey, and *perform* as a 'speech act' that expresses a desire to right the relationship damaged through the actions of the apologizer . . . It clears or 'settles' the air in order to begin reconstructing the broken connections between two human beings."[19] Or as Stefaans Coetzee (a member of the Afrikaner Resistance Movement convicted of killing four people and injuring sixty-seven others in a bomb attack) came to realize, saying sorry isn't enough. "There must be doing of sorry."[20]

What might "doing of sorry" entail? It begins with an honest naming of and reckoning with the past. Tutu put it plainly: "True forgiveness deals with the past, all of the past, to make the future possible." And again: "True reconciliation exposes the awfulness, the abuse, the pain, the hurt, the truth."[21] If people fail to investigate the past, they will fail to notice how past structures and patterns of behaving are still influencing and operating in the present and thus not have a clear understanding of what needs to change. But dealing with *all* the past is not easily done, especially when recalling it brings people face to face with histories of violence and neglect. As numerous scholars have noted, people find it hard to live honestly with themselves. They prefer to repeat to themselves and to others stories about the past that cast them in a good or at least acceptable light. The impulse reverberates in the cultural liturgies that perpetuate myths of a community's or nation's innocent and glorious past.[22] But the impulse also resounds in individuals, as Jacqueline Rose observes: "Our minds are endlessly engaged in the business of tidying up the landscape of the heart so that . . . we can feel better about ourselves." This strategy is dangerous because it depends on people denying or distorting their histories. In this denial and distortion they (a) lie about the pain and suffering circulating through the world and (b) refuse to acknowledge their role in perpetuating, whether intentionally or not, that pain and suffering. When people repudiate their role in the creation and perpetuation of brutality in the world, they grant violence "its license to roam, since it then becomes essential that someone else bear the responsibility, shoulder the burden, pay the price."[23]

The doing of sorry continues with the work of correcting the systems and behaviors that bring about pain and suffering. Apology needs to be accompanied by accountability on the part of those admitting injustice. They must pledge themselves to work for a more just and reconciled world.[24] Krog insists that "forgiveness can never be without the next step—reconciliation—and reconciliation cannot take place unless it fundamentally changes the life of the one that forgave as well as the forgiven one."[25]

As the TRC was concluding its work, Tutu understood

that there can be no real healing or reconciliation apart from a commitment to rehabilitation and reparation.[26] Reparations are crucial today and always because they focus on the systems and infrastructures that continue to harm people. After decades of promoting evil policies, the South African government must now put its effort and resources toward building an equitable society in which all people have access to land, housing, education, health care, food, and legal representation. To refuse to repair the structures that perpetuate harm is to refuse to extend a helping hand. Here again, the ubuntu underpinnings of Tutu's way of thinking need to be borne in mind: to build a hopeful future, a society's leaders must work with all its members to create healthy and just communities in which the maximum flourishing of all their members becomes possible.

Gobodo-Madikizela recognizes that "reconciliation has become a dirty word, and some people see it as a masquerade for impunity." But she also insists that we not forgo the work of reconciliation, which "shifts from an exclusive focus on prosecutions to allow the emergence of a profoundly new politics of engagement with the past, not in order to rekindle old hatreds, but to learn from them."[27] Others, quite rightly, are suspicious about the purveyors of reconciliation because they sense in these gestures a desire to forget the past and deny its continuing (often wicked) influence in contemporary affairs.[28] But as Gobodo-Madikizela has observed, a spirit of forgiveness and a yearning for reconciliation unleash a powerful presence in the world: the desire to build a future based on mercy and compassion and rooted in the understanding that all people are worthy of being loved, even when they behave badly. In the midst of pain and acrimony, forgiveness allows, even prompts, the imagination to see a different way of being. "Our capacity for such empathy is a profound gift in this brutal world we have created for one another."[29]

Krog recognized the biggest failure of the TRC: it did not secure for South Africans the degree of reparation that victims were owed. Far from it. The South African government was repeatedly told that repair and redress of unjust structures was the axis on which a hopeful South Africa moved, but it did not heed the TRC's recommendations. The youth of South Africa are still waiting for government and community leaders to address the pressing concerns the TRC raised.[30] Despite this failure on the part of the South African government, Tutu says, "I want to assert as eloquently and as passionately as I can that it [i.e., the work of the TRC] was, in an imperfect world, the best possible instrument so far devised to deal with the kind of situation that confronted us after democracy was established in our motherland. With all its imperfections, what we have tried to do in South Africa has attracted the attention of the world. This tired, disillusioned, cynical world, hurting so frequently and so grievously, has marveled at a process that holds out considerable hope in the midst of much that negates hope."[31]

7
A Hopeful Architecture

In the concluding lines of "The Hell of Treblinka," one of the first published essays on the Nazi death camps, Vasily Grossman wrote that lovers of humanity must always bear a simple truth in mind: "It is possible to demonstrate with nothing more than a pencil that any large construction company with experience in the use of reinforced concrete can, in the course of six months and with a properly organized labor force, construct more than enough chambers to gas the entire population of the earth." Construction workers didn't need much time to build a factory of death. They didn't need much space either: "Ten small chambers—hardly enough space, if properly furnished, to stable a hundred horses—ten such chambers turned out to be enough to kill three million people."[1]

The architectures of terror, dehumanization, and killing were remarkably easy to build. Several of the characteristics prized by modern technocrats—precise calculation and control, maximization of yield, and machine efficiency—were put to work in the camp's design, construction, and operation. Surveying the facilities, Grossman was struck by how much the layout and the buildings followed the principles of any large-scale modern industrial enterprise. Reading the reports of the few survivors, and thereby learning about the design elements that maximized brutality and violence, he was shocked by the efficiency with which the structure itself enabled the demonic work of the camp.

We might dismiss Grossman's description of Treblinka as an isolated and especially egregious manifestation of the architecture of hell. We shouldn't. Grossman was a war correspondent for the Russian army newspaper *Red Star.* He traveled across much of Europe to witness and report the living conditions of millions. The brutality he observed at Treblinka was not confined to one location, he realized, nor was it a complete aberration. It was a logical extension of decades-old principles and policies that had the support of captains of industry and political elites. He knew that the fascism gripping Europe did not appear out of nowhere. When Viktor Pavlovich Shtrum, one of the main characters in Grossman's 1952 novel *Stalingrad,* asked, "Who has turned the whole of Europe into a huge concentration camp?" Grossman was making a crucial philosophical point: a morbidly sick culture creates a built environment that degrades and destroys life. When people are consigned to live and work in soul-alienating and soul-brutalizing farms, apartments, cities, mines, and factories, the sickness becomes endemic.[2]

In *Everything Flows,* his last novel, Grossman described how "the spirit of the camp" infused almost every aspect of the Soviet world. "Barbed wire, it seemed, was no longer necessary; life outside the barbed wire had become, in its essence, no different from that of the barracks."[3] Though Soviet leaders trumpeted their great military victories, their massive construction sites, the creation of cities from scratch, canals that joined sea to sea, the collectivization of farms, the mechanization of production, and their enormous energy projects, the Russian people lived in perpetual fear of the Gulag.[4] "From the Pacific Ocean to the Black Sea, non-freedom triumphed—everywhere and in everything. Everywhere and in everything, freedom was killed." To accomplish Lenin's and Stalin's revolutionary aims, untold numbers of people had to be shot, tortured, starved, displaced, and incarcerated. The Soviet world had little room for kindness, intimacy, or responsibility, little genuine sociality, little free disagreement, and little creative life. "Freedom, after all, is life; to overcome freedom, Stalin had to kill life."[5]

Beneath the many assaults on freedom Grossman saw that a spirit of contempt ruled and was enforced by violence. Though some people might be so fortunate as to have a memory of beauty or a dream of compassionate touch, most people now inhabited a world governed by what one of his characters, Aleksy Samoilovich, called "the law of the conservation of violence."

> It's as simple as the law of the conservation of energy. Violence is eternal, no matter what is done to destroy it. It does not disappear or diminish; it can only change shape. It can be embodied in slavery, or in the Mongol invasion. It wanders from continent to continent. Sometimes it takes the form of class struggle, sometimes a race struggle. From the sphere of the material it slips into religiosity, as in the Middle Ages. Sometimes it is directed against colored people, sometimes against writers and artists, but, all in all, the total quantity of violence on earth remains constant. Thinkers mistake its constant chaotic transformations for evolution and search for its laws. But chaos knows no laws, no evolution, no meaning, and no aim.[6]

We could disagree with Samoilovich about whether violence is an eternal or constant quantity, but he clearly had ample material evidence to support the claim that violence wanders across the globe, takes many economic and architectural forms, and can be directed against anyone.

The severity of this law cannot be adequately appreciated until we understand that violence is a material structure and not only an event. A spirit of violence isn't simply active *on* a world. It becomes built into it, with the result that the life that grows out of that world is either stunted, distorted, or destroyed. Geography itself—for example, the quality of neighborhoods and workplaces, the prevalence of health-care and educational facilities, and the availability of affordable transportation and energy networks—perpetuates ways of being that either frustrate or cherish life, that either keep people apart or bring them together. As Katherine McKittrick observed, no place "just is" a static and neutral backdrop. Built environments always encode a framework of meanings and values. They give material expression to what their builders think is important and to a vision of how life should be ordered and arranged. As a consequence, they also structure the kinds of relationships that will happen. Racism and sexism are not simply bodily or identity-based realities. They are "spatial acts" that isolate, segregate, degrade, violate, and abandon.[7] In short, what we build in the world communicates what we think of the world and what we value about its inhabitants.

Consider some of the defining material structures and habitats of the modern world.

- the slave ships and auction blocks that served the plantations that brutalized lands and people
- the reservations that confine Indigenous peoples to lands deemed undesirable
- the enclosure and privatization of lands traditionally held in common

- the "sacrifice zones" controlled by mining companies that decimate local communities and leave behind toxic waste
- the land grabs by foreign governments and wealthy elites
- the massive hydroelectric projects that, by damming rivers, displace Indigenous communities and dramatically alter ecosystems
- the mountaintop removal sites where mountaintops are systematically blasted away to provide access to seams of coal
- the vast fields of monoculture agriculture that depend on toxic herbicides and synthetic fertilizers to maximize production
- the large confinement animal feeding operations (CAFOs) that degrade livestock and pollute surrounding watersheds and lands
- the "cancer alleys" where people live on lands and along waterways polluted by the toxic chemicals of industrial production
- the public housing projects that consign residents to inhumane living conditions
- the appearance of massive slums in the world's growing megacities that lack the basic infrastructure to meet the health, educational, and work needs of its residents
- the many "camps"—work camps, death camps, prisoner-of-war camps, internment camps, refugee resettlement camps—constructed in contexts of war, political persecution, and climate instability

This list is not meant to deny the construction of many beautiful, inspiring, and life-giving structures. I highlight these sites, however, because they are not created accidentally, nor are they located on the periphery of cities and states. They are foundational structures upon which the modern world is built and continues to develop.

Too much of the geography of modernity communicates what the varying resonance-destroying desires to control and appropriate the world have created: built environments that harm ecosystems and the people who inhabit them. The colonial and industrial enterprises that gave birth to and continue to sustain modern economies have resulted in a desacralized world in which few places are cherished or deemed worthy of our devotion and care. In this world, fellow creatures (human and nonhuman) have been reduced to units of production and consumption and thus cannot signify as either kin or companions in a shared life. In today's global order, as Achille Mbembe has observed, old colonial divisions "have been replaced with various forms of apartheid, marginalization, and structural destitution. Global processes of accumulation and expropriation in an increasingly brutal world economic system have created new forms of violence and inequality." The aims of the dominant economies of our time, and the designs of the environments built to maximize these aims, do not have as their first priority "the possibility for subjects to stand up, walk with their own feet, use their own hands, faces, and bodies to write their own histories as part of a world that we all share, to which we all have a right, to which we are all heirs."[8]

Outlining this grim geography alerts us to the state of the world the young people of our time are inheriting from us: a world considerably diminished in fertility, biodiversity, and healthiness. They are being asked to imagine their future in a world that is increasingly wounded, polluted, ugly, and uninhabitable, a world with built environments that do not facilitate the mutual flourishing of people and places together. Can we ask people to live in hope if their homes and places of work do not nurture and celebrate life?

The defining built environments we have today were not inevitable. Historically, cultures around the world have built homes and farms and designed neighborhoods and villages that respected and honored life. They have not always fully succeeded, but in their efforts they have taught us a great deal about the enduring design elements that foster health and inspire the creation of beauty. What are the principles that create an architecture in which hope can grow?

In *The Timeless Way of Building*, the architect and builder Christopher Alexander, along with a team of colleagues, set out to distill the design principles that have proven themselves over time and across cultures to promote the flourishing of communities wherever they are located. They wanted first to identify the built environments that promoted maximal "aliveness" in community members and then to delineate the multiple material and philosophical elements that brought these environments into being. Their starting premise, as Alexander put it, was simple: "We can come alive only to the extent the buildings and towns we live in are alive." The varying states of alienation, ennui, and despair that Alexander saw in modern societies, and the sorry state of many of the built environments their members inhabited, convinced him that neither designers nor residents appreciated the close connection between architecture and human well-being. "In a world which is healthy, whole, alive, and self-maintaining, people themselves can be alive and self-creating. In a world which is unwhole and self-destroying, people cannot be alive: they will inevitably themselves be self-destroying, and miserable."[9]

Sheltering and nurturing aliveness is the fundamental principle that guides Alexander's design commitments. To appreciate how radical his commitments are, we need to understand how deadness has been the framing assumption in much modern building. As numerous historians have noted, European encounters with Indigenous peoples revealed fundamentally different ways of perceiving and engaging the world. Where natives (but also many traditional agricultural peoples in Europe) saw the land as alive and ever prone to fresh and diverse expressions of life, European explorers and conquerors saw inert land without any vitality or purpose of its own. It is precisely the idea that the whole of nature is dead, a mere collection of objects, that underwrites the many modern projects to conquer, control, commodify, privatize, modify, and engineer forests, fields, and watersheds—along with their many diverse plant and animal creatures—to the owner's liking. As Amitav Ghosh makes painfully clear, exploration and conquest required a massive effort that depended on ruthless violence for its success. "These conjoined processes of violence, physical and intellectual, were all necessary for the emergence of a new economy based on extracting resources from a desacralized, inanimate Earth."[10]

A world reduced to a resource, ready to be exploited, is a world without meaning of its own. Whatever value things have depends entirely on the value people assign to them. This world lacks the freshness, vitality, and sanctity that might otherwise inspire people to build an abiding and cherished home, to establish a cultivated place in which kinship relations are honored and celebrated because they are the indispensable condition of a dynamic, verdant, and ever-fresh life. A dead world, in other words, does not inspire reverence or delight. It doesn't resonate. Nor can people be content for long within it. Instead, it breeds various forms of restlessness, alienation, and contempt that, ultimately, leave people feeling abandoned, alone, and perhaps even contemptible themselves.[11] People fool themselves if they think they can affirm their own worth by rendering worthless the places and fellow creatures upon which they daily depend. The nurturing of people presupposes the nurturing of the places through which they construct their lives.

Aliveness, like beauty, is not a quality that can be fully comprehended or succinctly expressed. It is not to be equated with existence, since we know that it is possible to "exist" while being "dead" to neighbors and neighborhood. What is clear is that the relationships happening in spaces that are alive are deeply resonant. Aliveness is never simply one thing or expressed in one mode. Because it is finely attuned to place, it can be calm and stormy, or tidy and spontaneous. Among its defining features, however, is the freedom and serenity that arise from the absence of conflicting and contradictory elements within it. People who are deeply alive are at peace with themselves and their neighbors. They are at rest and feel contentment even while being active, even while struggling from time to time. They are not driven by the ego that needs to assert or impose itself on others and that secures its worth by acquiring more and more space. Their comfort and joy are to be in the presence of and in harmony with others. They do not want to control others, since the exercise of control invariably distorts and diminishes who the others are. Their feeling of aliveness increases because they feel themselves to be part of a relational whole in which members constantly receive from and respond to others. To be in a place of belonging, nurture, and affirmation is to be alive.

Indigenous peoples did not encounter their invaders as "alive" in the sense I have just described. Instead, they met people who were animated by violent strife, strife against the world but also within themselves. In *History of the New World,* written by the Italian conquistador Girolamo Benzoni and published in 1565, Benzoni describes what Indigenous people thought of their invaders: "They say we have come to this earth to destroy the world. They say . . . that we devour everything, we consume the earth, we redirect the rivers, we are never quiet, never at rest, but always run here and there, seeking gold and silver, never satisfied, and then we gamble with it, make war, kill each other, rob, swear, never say the truth, and have deprived them of their means of livelihood."[12] The existence of these invaders could scarcely be in doubt, since they so often left a trail of destruction in their wake. But were they alive? Did they desire the sabbath rest that orients proper dwelling on this earth?

If people deeply alive have a distinct way of perceiving and engaging their world, they will also build differently. Rather than simply imposing a design on a place, they will take the time to listen and be attentive to the place and to assess its potential before working with it, all so that the place and its creatures can fully and freely express themselves. The key is to come to an awareness of the inner nature of things by asking what this place or creature can become if the conditions are right for its optimal growth and development. It is to ask how I, as a member of this living and dynamic whole, can participate in the flows and processes of life that are already at work here. Alexander describes this as humanity's participation in the natural unfolding of things, meaning by "nature" and "natural" those things "which are perfectly reconciled with their own inner forces."[13] Taking this approach means that "we can only make a building live when we are egoless."[14]

Alexander believes that a commitment to aliveness, though perhaps not regularly thematized, has been assumed and put to work by many cultures in their diverse building efforts. Throughout history people have constructed implements and rooms, built houses and workshops, and designed neighborhoods and villages so they can feel at home in their world. A home or a neighborhood is not simply a location. It is a dynamic place where the energy of its co-inhabitants is respected and nurtured and where all who live there feel the energy of the place flowing through them. It is a place where work and play, individual and social time, security and daring, shelter and openness come together. A home makes room for surprises and for strangers, and for the trepidations and tensions that invariably accompany encounters with the unknown. It is not a fortress to keep others out, or a vacuum to suck everything in while giving nothing back (because things are never isolated naturally but are instead dynamically and organically connected to others). What homes and neighborhoods do is give people a place from which to grow outward and alongside others, all the while seeking ever-greater coherence and ever-deeper harmony: "when you build a thing you cannot merely build that thing in isolation, but must also repair the world around it, so that the larger world at one place becomes more coherent, and more whole; and the thing which you make takes its place in the web of nature, as you make it."[15]

As Alexander and his team traveled around the world they searched for the patterns and design elements that govern the construction of healthy living places, ranging from the layout and optimal size of towns to the placing of windows and sitting spaces in homes. They noted the importance of public spaces and town squares for spontaneous and relaxed encounters between people. They highlighted the value of public access to green spaces and the role that sacred sites play in creating a sense of community and shared life. They noted the design elements (parks, town squares, bandstands, wide boulevards) that facilitated "dancing in the streets" and observed that in more modern and technologically advanced societies, communities were more fragmented (roads and cars had much to do with that) and that people there felt more uncomfortable walking on streets and encountering strangers. Having distilled their findings into 253 patterns, they concluded that urban sprawl is detrimental to well-being because it fragments neighborhoods, isolates people, and bars access to natural habitats and wildlife. The best cities create multiple opportunities for people of diverse ages and backgrounds to engage with each other in their work and play. The best buildings are not enormous and undifferentiated but make room for multiple spaces in which people can meet, interact, and express themselves.

Another way to describe Alexander's design ambitions is to say that he wants to construct places in which "love's braided dance" can occur, a dance that is between people but also between people and fellow creatures and their shared places. Urban planners have pursued similar aims in their desire to build what have been called "Twenty- or Fifteen-Minute Neighborhoods," places that put people in walking proximity with each other and with various amenities like shops, schools, eateries, health-care facilities, green spaces, recreational parks, community centers, and entertainment venues. People have grown tired of sprawling, car-dependent spaces that segregate life's functions and that leave people feeling isolated and alone. They are asking for high-quality housing and beautiful public places that maximize personal encounters and that promote physical and mental health.

Neighborhoods are at their best when area residents come together to decide how to make public spaces safe and likely to inspire mutual flourishing. The goal of what is often called asset-based community development (ABCD) is to create built environments that facilitate quality relationships in which people get to know each other and become a source of help to each other. Public benches, parks, and squares are often prominent in these neighborhoods because they encourage people to linger and spend time with each other. They also create a sense of belonging as people share news and information about opportunities available in their area. One of the clearest signs of a vibrant and healthy neighborhood is that people of all ages, along with their strollers, wheelchairs, and walkers, are found safely and comfortably moving within its spaces. When this happens, architects fulfill what the philosopher Alan de Botton says is architecture's most important task, which is "to render vivid to us who we might ideally be."[16]

Rwanda might seem an unlikely place to see several hope-inducing design elements at work. A lush country located in the Great Rift Valley of central Africa, Rwanda is remembered by many as the site of the 1994 genocide in which over half a million Tutsis were killed by Hutu militias. Rwanda's economy was severely affected by the bloodshed. Much of the infrastructure that subsistence farmers needed to maintain their living was destroyed. But Rwanda is being reborn. Reductions in poverty and mortality have been profound. Biodiversity is increasing, and urban spaces now feature public gardens, genocide memorials, and clean streets.

One of Rwanda's most inspiring buildings is not in the capital city of Kigali. It is in Butaro, a small village in one of the most remote and underserved regions of Rwanda. Here, atop a hill overlooking rich agricultural lands, sits a hospital that was designed to cultivate the dignity of persons and celebrate the beauty of the region. Dr. Agnes Binagwaho, a former minister of health of Rwanda and currently the vice-chancellor of the University of Global Health Equity, says, "When we look at the hospital, we cannot help but admire its beauty. And the structure itself is as beautiful as the mission it embraces. It is a deeper beauty that provides everyone with what they deserve as human beings. A beauty that makes us better. A beauty that draws out of us the best things within and inspires us to give our best."[17]

Upon entering the hospital grounds, a visitor is immediately struck by the lush vegetation, the flower gardens, and the centering presence of a large *umuvumu* tree. This species of tree, which serves as a traditional gathering place in Rwandan culture, communicates that the hospital is a place in which people are meant to find solace, support, and companionship. The vegetation isn't simply decorative: green spaces are known to reduce stress and pain perception in patients. Patients and their families are encouraged to spend time outside because fresh air spaces reduce the spread of airborne disease. Paths, benches, and covered informal sitting areas dot the grounds for this reason.

The buildings are not ornate. Simple yet elegant lines communicate flow. White walls inside and out create a bright atmosphere that contrasts attractively with the locally sourced wood trim and the volcanic rock that has been fitted together like so many intricate jigsaw puzzles. Numerous large windows look out onto pastoral scenes in the valley below, while corridors surround the perimeters of buildings to heighten the sense of sociability. When patients come to this hospital, they are meant to feel and know through the architecture that they are not alone but are surrounded by the healing powers of community and nature.

The creation of beauty should not be reserved for the wealthy few. Nor should beauty be seen as an optional luxury or an occasional means to alleviate the ugliness that might otherwise define our places. As Binagwaho understands it,

> When we put people in an ugly, uninspiring place, we are conveying that they deserve something less than the best . . . when we put people in a beautiful environment—and one that they had a voice in creating—then it is only natural that we will create a community which is ready to cultivate solidarity and equity . . . We know that the environment has

> an impact on health outcomes and believe that if we are not able to improve the places where we work, then it will be difficult to improve the way we work.[18]

Michael Murphy, one of the architects enlisted to design the hospital, elaborates:

> The work and toil and maintenance that creates beauty produces a profound sense of worth. Human dignity, that feeling that we matter, that someone has noticed me for who I am, is found in those processes of beautification, the tending of the garden, the discovery that a building's design locates us in a place, that we are respected for who we are. Dignity navigates the oscillation between *me* and *we*. The construction of dignity erodes the false dichotomy [that compels people to choose between justice and beauty].[19]

Why is this hospital beautiful when so many of the health-care facilities in Africa are poorly designed and cheaply built? At other hospitals a visitor regularly encounters rooms and hallways that are grim and dark, patterned as they often are on nineteenth-century European sanatoria that were built to isolate patients from each other. The problem isn't simply that a lack of funding results in unclean, unlovely, underequipped, and understaffed facilities. The problem goes deeper, into the heart of the architectural design process itself. When Binagwaho selected the architects who would work on this hospital, she chose young architects who would not be beholden to established conventions, processes, and forms; indeed, the design group eventually coalesced to become MASS, which stands for Model of Architecture Serving Society. Murphy was part of the original MASS group, as was Alan Ricks. What they did not realize was that their training at Harvard University's School of Design did not prepare them adequately to design the hospital as it was conceived. Like many schools of architectural design, Harvard emphasized schematic design, construction documents, building plans, and contract administration. As Ricks later observed, little in this education spoke of community health, community needs, or the ability of a community to contribute to the building of its own structures.

The first attempt to design the hospital was a failure. The design didn't grow out of or celebrate Butaro and its people. It consisted of multiple elements chosen from a standardized list of building options that were then imposed on the site. Murphy and Ricks soon realized that they would need to move to Butaro, get to know the people and the region, and engage local people in the hospital's design and construction. The mental shift required was profound and enduring because they needed to resist a scarcity mindset and stop assuming there wasn't enough money, labor, equipment, supplies, or time to complete the project. "Perhaps the most fundamental shift," says Ricks, "was to change our preconceptions about resource limitation, and instead to look at the opportunities that abound when you are present and proximate, rather than airdropping in a prefabricated solution."[20]

Officials from every level of government, along with thousands of area residents, were involved in the construction of the hospital. Thousands of jobs were created as people dug the foundations, erected the walls, did the stonework, built the furniture and trim, and established the gardens and walkways. Once the hospital was built, hundreds more jobs were created to keep the facility going. Eighty-five percent of the building costs were invested in the local economy. The people who were going to be served by the hospital also had a direct say in how it was to look and feel. They insisted on creating several places for people to gather comfortably and on ensuring lots of natural light and fresh air movement inside the buildings. The facility, nearly 65,000 square feet in capacity, houses 150 beds (each looking out onto the Rwandan countryside), inpatient and outpatient services, a laboratory, maternity care facilities, operating rooms, and a neonatal intensive care unit. Buildings are constantly evolving as people see where improvements can be made. A successful building honors its place and meets the needs of those who will use it. A single design cannot simply be exported from place to place. It must be created anew, from the ground up and with the aid of the many hands and thoughts of those who will live in and with it.

When people come to the hospital, they do not merely enter a beautiful and well-equipped facility. They see and touch a collection of buildings that reflect back to them the love, creativity, skill, and devotion that they, family members, and friends have invested in their construction. They see a place that has been created out of friendship and that honors the place and its people. They take pride in the fact that so many women and young people learned the skills of design and construction on the job and now have taken those skills to start their own businesses. Members of the community feel a deep sense of responsibility for the hospital because the community was involved from the beginning in its design and construction.

Binagwaho understood from the start that this project "must involve the people we are serving in shaping their own future. Every stone on this campus represents the work done by this community to build a better future."[21] Community members also take pride in the garden that sits at the center of the hospital and that celebrates the vegetation of the region. As the master gardener Jean Baptiste Maniragaba sees it, "The garden is essential to the building. When the building is finished, there must be a garden to make it beautiful. The trees bring fresh air, the flowers are beautiful and smell nice. Some of them are medicinal, some are pollen-rich for bees to make honey, some have a nice odor, and they each bring out the best in the landscape. And that makes me happy. Beauty brings joy to life." When he works in the garden and engages people he meets, he regularly exclaims, "*Nziza Cyane,*" which variously translates as "very good," "something is making you happy," or "healing landscape."[22]

As the hospital in Butaro demonstrates, every building tells a story that communicates what people think of their place and community and what values and goals they think most important to realize. Too much architecture has put financial profits (for some) ahead of the health of a place and its people. The result has been built environments and structures that are ugly, dangerous, and soul-destroying, the kinds of places that instill hopelessness. The unnecessary and non-inevitable creation of hopelessness should concern us because, as Bryan Stevenson regularly notes in his public presentations, "Hopelessness is the enemy of justice." As Butaro also shows, justice is created as people focus on designing and building shared places that nurture life. Working together, not just on hospitals but on schools, homes, parks, transportation networks, and places of work, enables people to feel more fully alive, more deeply appreciated and honored. They just might feel inspired to dance.

People do not need to choose between beauty and justice. They can pursue both in the construction of buildings that honor their community and celebrate their place in it. Looking at the hospital today, Binagwaho says, "We refused to let that dark past [of the genocide] define us or our future . . . It is necessary to give people the possibility to dream . . . The biggest handicap in life is the failure of imagination. We dreamt of a beautiful future; Butaro District Hospital and the University of Global Health Equity are proof that great dreams are possible."[23]

A hopeful architecture communicates that people and places are worthy of care and respect. By reflecting a loving intention in their design and construction, neighborhoods and buildings convey that the people who work and play and rest there are also loved. Hopeful ways of being need homes, workplaces, gathering and recreational spaces, sacred sites, and farm fields and forests that say life is precious and that it will be protected, nurtured, and celebrated.

8
A Hopeful Economy

In the opening lines of *The Theory of Moral Sentiments,* Adam Smith says, "How selfish soever man may be supposed, there are evidently some principles in his nature, which interest him in the fortunes of others, and render their happiness necessary to him, though he derives nothing from it, except the pleasure of seeing it." In other words, the happiness of others doesn't simply matter as an occasional or accidental benefit. Rather, it is a necessity, which is why people should work for the good of others, even if that pursuit is of no practical benefit to them. Pity and compassion are natural responses to the experience of misery, and people feel sorrow, too, when they encounter it in others. This feeling for others is so deeply implanted within us, says Smith, that even "the greatest ruffian, the most hardened violator of the laws of society, is not altogether without it."[1]

The trouble, however, is that "we have no immediate experience of what other men feel." Though we might see a brother in torment, "as long as we ourselves are at our ease, our senses will never inform us of what he suffers." For this reason, Smith called on people to cultivate an "imaginative sympathy," to put themselves in another person's shoes and thereby learn to feel something of what that person feels. The intimacy of feeling he seeks is striking. "By the imagination we place ourselves in his situation, we conceive ourselves enduring all the same torments, we enter as it were into his body, and become in some measure the same person with him, and thence form some idea of his sensations, and even feel something which, though weaker in degree, is not altogether unlike them. His agonies, when they are thus brought home to ourselves, when we have thus adopted and made them our own, begin at last to affect us, and we then tremble and shudder at the thought of what he feels."[2]

Smith's desire to foster among people "a mutual sympathy of sentiments" might surprise us, given his often-quoted line (from *The Wealth of Nations*): "It is not from the benevolence of the butcher, the brewer, or the baker that we expect our dinner, but from their regard to their own interest." It shouldn't, for as the historian and political scientist Corey Robin has noted, "The idea of the market as a communion of souls was once the lingua franca of European culture, helping to midwife the birth of economics from the seventeenth to the eighteenth centuries. Commerce was seen as a source of sociability, pulling solitary selves out of isolation, drawing far-flung communities into contact with each other." By addressing mutual needs and facilitating the sharing of resources, markets can bring people together, deepening their sympathies, broadening their perspectives, and making their understanding more cosmopolitan. That's the argument. David Hume, one of Smith's more influential friends, went so far as to suggest that the more an economy developed, "the more sociable men become."[3]

It didn't turn out quite that way, at least not in many of the places Smith's thinking went to work. Robin puts the matter succinctly: "Once upon a time, economics and sympathy were one and the same . . . [But] something got lost on the way to the market." Though the promise of commerce may have been "to lure isolated communities to a greater mutuality, the practice of international trade produced the opposite: the degradation, domination, and murder of non-Europeans."[4] The practices of industrial production at home and abroad, the colonial drive to commodify and extract natural wealth from across the globe, the displacement and genocide of Indigenous populations, and the enslavement of millions of workers killed sympathy, or at least severely curtailed its reach. If Smith's desire was for people to draw so near to others as to feel in their bodies whatever agonies others may be feeling, the effect of the markets he helped create was to inflict agonies upon them he might hardly have imagined.

Of course, the story is more complicated than the brief distillation that Robin offers. Modern economic forms produced multiple genuine goods and services, including for some (mostly European, mostly white) populations that were better fed and better clothed, lived longer, resided in more comfortable housing, had increased access to medical care, and had more opportunities for leisure activities. The specialization that Smith's butchers, brewers, and bakers represent often had the effect of making the meat, beer, and bread they produced more available, cheaper, and of higher quality. Not all economic benefits were equally distributed, but their admittedly partial and imperfect realization meant that a growing number of people could now imagine a life that was safer and more comfortable.

My aim is not to suggest that all self-interest is wicked or that markets are evil. It is to explore what an economy would look like if sympathy for each other and our shared places inspired and animated it. Sympathy is the indispensable foundation upon which love flourishes. It is not an overlay but the core of the relations that we *are* rather than merely *have*. The designer and philosopher Lars Spuybroek puts it this way: "Sympathy is not something extra, added on top of our relations with things and with each other; rather, *it lies at the core of those relations*. Sympathy is the very stuff relations are made of . . . Sympathy is the power of things at work, working between all things, and between us and things."[5]

Etymologically speaking, an "eco-nomy" is the way households / families / home places (*oikos*) are governed (*nomos*) by people. A sympathetic economy would therefore be one in which people are committed to building worlds and promoting processes that help people and places fit and flourish together. The activation of sympathy is critical to this effort because it is the affective capacity that joins people to each other and their shared places, enabling each person to be a nurturing, creative, healing, and celebratory presence where they work and live. Sympathy is the skilled and disciplined power that teaches people to respect the sanctity of others and to participate in the cultivation of a healthy and beautiful world. Simply put, an economy devoid of sympathy is an economy that degrades life and diminishes hope.

The idea of a sympathetic economy rests on a profound natural (non-conscious, non-affective) sympathy that is reflected in processes as basic as the capacity of soils, seeds, water, and weather to produce verdant plant life. The world we inhabit is not dead; it is not a mess of unrelated bits, a lifeless mechanism that moves as the effect of inscrutable algorithms. No. It is alive in ways that defy expectation and comprehension. Life is an ever-evolving reality in which creatures large and small are continually attracting, influencing, and ingesting each other and, in these mutual shaping and nurturing processes, generating fresh life. Sympathy is a conscious and felt capacity in people, but in the natural world sympathy is the ability of creatures to draw from and share life with each other, an ability reflected in processes like geological formation, decomposition, photosynthesis, reproduction, birth, digestion, growth, and pollination. This sympathy makes the world one lavish, symbiotic, and mysterious space of hospitality: a home and not merely an environment. In this home creatures alternate between playing host and guest to each other; they constantly receive from others what they need for their own development and constantly contribute to others what the others need for their development.

The natural processes enabling life to flourish are not mechanical. The component parts cannot be disassembled the way a mechanic can disassemble a once-running engine. Nature is more intimate than that. Things and creatures are continuously affecting and changing each other at the most visceral levels. We can observe this when we cook. Once salt enters a dish, the whole dish changes. Even if we could somehow remove the salt, the ingredients would not be restored to their original state. Ingredients, in other words, do not simply aggregate. They resonate and interpenetrate, and because they resonate, they can produce flavors and nutrition profiles that are surprising, delectable, and life-enhancing. Creatures, too, live only because they are constantly working themselves into the lives of others. Eating is the means and movement of life. To eat is to participate in processes that do not simply connect eater and eaten but braid them together. Neither could be what it is apart from the other. Sympathy is "what things feel when they shape each other."[6]

Characterizing earth as one vast kitchen, and life as the immensely complex and differentiated actions of cooking and eating, may seem a bit of a stretch. But the stretch is a small one. This characterization rightly points out that creatures are so intimately and irrevocably entangled in the lives of each other that we cannot make sense of them apart from their fellow creatures, the places they live, their histories together, and their visceral interconnections. People do not simply live *on* earth. More precisely, they are the embodied expressions of the earth living *through* them. Every time I take a bite, drink, or breath, the world, along with all the geo-bio-eco-social processes that make it flourish, enters deep inside me, affecting and nurturing me at the levels of respiration, digestion, mood, inspiration, and growth.

To say that the earth is our home is to describe a habitat or dwelling place—a noun. But a home also requires the many physiological processes that nurture the beings that live there and in which they participate—a verb. Homes can be messy and disagreeable, but we cannot live without them, not even for one moment. This is why our most important economic priority must be to nurture the earth and all the ecological and sociological processes that nurture us.

When sympathy erodes, the feel of life and the meaning of things change, along with what people think the aim of a life ought to be. To see what I mean, consider the life of Samuel Rockall, who was born in 1878 and died in 1962. Rockall was a woodman, sawyer, furniture maker, gardener, and fruit farmer. His primary occupation, however, was bodger—someone who makes chairs of beechwood. Rockall turned and shaved the beech trees of his neighborhood into beautifully crafted chairs. When H. J. Massingham visited his home and shop in the Chilterns region, northwest of London, in the early years of the twentieth century, Rockall told him that all the things he used carried memory and meaning. A jar of blackberry jam, for instance, evoked the brambles and bushes that grew the blackberries and the seasons that produced a fruiting plant. When he tasted the jam, he also tasted the skill and care that went into the making of each jarful. The shovel he used daily to garden and to clean up the shop was special because it held and reflected back to him the memory of forty years of use. When he looked at it, he also saw that his mending of it over the years had made it continuously useful. Rockall expressed real affection for this particular shovel not because it was perfect but because it had helped him make his home productive. In Massingham's estimation, what made Rockall's work so exemplary was that he placed himself as an intermediary between nature and society, seeking to honor each in the making of beautiful, tasty, nutritious, and useful things. "The craftsman knows nature *in the grain* and never goes against it. He has grasped essential structure in the substance."[7]

As Massingham reflected on his many visits he was struck by how the objects Rockall used were always more than simply themselves. Each carried "the wealth of associations that gathered round it."[8] When Rockall looked out onto his homeplace and when he worked with his tools, he felt a profound sense of connection and fit with the forces of life circulating through the land, through the trees, and through him. To be sure, life could be hard and frustrating. Nonetheless, his shop and his cottage made a good and pleasing home that elevated the significance of his work by linking it to the fertility, birth, growth, flowering, fruiting, dying, and decomposition unfolding all around him.

When Rockall worked in his shop, he certainly thought in terms of quantities and made calculations of varying sorts, as when he switched from using a pole lathe to a more muscle-efficient treadle lathe. His mind, however, was preoccupied with measures of quality: the fertility of his soils, the feel of a tool in his hand, the taste of his vegetables, and the look and comfort of his chairs. The elements that made up his home place could be numbered, but none was reducible to a number. To handle them with care and respect he had to attend to them as the unique things that they were. Frugality was at the heart of his work ethic. To waste anything was to disrespect the world that provided it. His frugality, however, was not experienced as deprivation because he understood how his garden, home, shop, and neighborhood made up an organic and meaningful whole of which he was an integral part. He didn't obsess over acquiring more because he appreciated and loved what he had. At Rockall's place, wrote Massingham,

> Nothing is wasted; everything turns into something else. Just as nothing is lost in Nature, so with Samuel. The trees he has axed come from the wood; they make multiform objects of use and beauty, while the shavings feed the hearth of home and the fertility of the garden. The transformation both of garden and wild maintain his family and preserve his independence. Trade, family, economy, livelihood, work, utility, ornament, all are parts of one organic whole . . . Nature is the source of his industry and each gains by the enrichment of the other. The great primaries of life—Nature, the home, the family, the craft, the land—share an intimate and mutual relation without losing their separate identities. Each is seen to be necessary to the other in the fulfillment of an integrated life. Use and beauty here have no quarrel any more than the wild with the domestic.[9]

I suspect that many people will find Rockall's world provincial and his way of life uncompelling. My aim in presenting it is not to turn back the clock, call people back to the land, or suggest that a crafting culture is uniformly idyllic. My aim is, instead, to testify to a way of life in which sympathy was active and determinative, however imperfectly, and which was productive of profound personal satisfaction, however mundane. Rockall knew that his way of working was on the way out and that his chairs, however lovingly and expertly created, could not ultimately compete with the machine-manufactured, cheaply priced chairs coming out of factories scattered about the globe. He also saw that a growing number of people were losing interest in village life.

In 1903 the German sociologist and philosopher Georg Simmel published an essay entitled "The Metropolis and Mental Life." In it he set out to describe the changes in sympathies that were occurring in Europe as great numbers of people moved from rural to urban settings. He wanted to know how relatively new economic forms of daily life—especially the increased reliance on money these forms required—were affecting how people thought about the world and their place within it. He noted that in village contexts, like Rockall's, life moved more slowly than in larger urban areas and was governed by personal relationships and emotional attachments. Folks tended to stay in the regions of their birth, so they came to know their homeplace geographies with a particularizing knowledge and their community members with a measure of intimacy. Village life was not perfect. Individuals regularly chafed under the yoke of social customs and the dictates of authority figures, both of which often stifled exploration, innovation, and freedom of expression.

Upon entering city spaces and assuming factory and office styles of work, wage laborers were often overwhelmed by the fast pace of life, the impersonality of encounters, and the amount and diversity of stimulation they encountered. In these new places of unfamiliarity and anonymity—products and people came from places that were mostly unknown—newcomers instinctively sought to protect themselves from the solicitation overload. They did this by developing what Simmel called an "essentially intellectualistic character," one that is much more rationalistic and calculating in its operations than was typical for village dwellers.[10] The key to survival was to desensitize, to minimize emotional attachments, and to become more reserved in relationships with others.

The desensitizing, or what may better be described as the growing impersonalization of life, took a variety of forms, but one of the most important centered on the transformation of work. In his magisterial work *The Philosophy of Money* (first published in Germany in 1910), Simmel noted that longstanding craft traditions of work facilitated a personal relationship between people and the things they owned because the producer's investment in the thing that was made transferred into an investment in the person for whom it was made. The difference is obvious when comparing a suit pulled off a rack to a suit made by a tailor. That's the consumer side of things. On the producer side, an impersonal ethos is also evident in the subdivisions of work and a reliance on machine technologies. The more the item made depends on a multitude of specialized parts, each made separately by a different machine, the less workers are able to express their personality through it. To appreciate the difference, contrast an item made with hand tools to an item made with a complex set of machines: "the specialization of tools paralyzes the effectiveness of personal qualities."[11] How would our world be different if the many things made or manufactured in it embodied their makers' devotion and commitment to beauty and durability?

My point is not to turn back the clock, eliminate all machine production, or suggest that the complete elimination of feeling has occurred in modern urban societies. Rather, it is to highlight an important shift in the character of the relationships between people and between people and things. The various forms of alienation, impersonality, and disenchantment described by Simmel, Marx, and Weber indicate the erosion of felt sympathies such that other people, things, and places are perceived as autonomous objects that stand apart from and sometimes against us. In this world resonance is hard to come by.

In the urban context Simmel analyzed, money became the indispensable means for negotiating daily life. People worked to make money to buy the things they needed to live. Simmel noted that the more people relied on money, however, the more matter-of-fact their relationships to people and to things became. Money changed how people thought about things: "Money is concerned only with what is common to all, i.e., with the exchange value which reduces all quality and individuality to a purely quantitative level. All emotional relationships between persons rest on their individuality, whereas intellectual relationships deal with persons as with numbers." Echoing the sentiment of Seneca, who—eighteen centuries earlier—said, "We no longer ask what things are but what they cost," Simmel noted how "money takes the place of all the manifoldness of things and expresses all qualitative distinctions between them in the distinction of 'how much.' To the extent that money, with its colorlessness and its indifferent quality, can become a common denominator of all values it becomes the frightful leveler—it hollows out the core of things, their peculiarities, their specific values and their uniqueness and incomparability in a way which is beyond repair." Simmel observed that as people take up a rationalistic, bureaucratic, calculating way of relating to others, they also develop what he called a "blasé attitude." The essence of this attitude was "an indifference toward the distinctions between things."[12] Indifference to things precludes sympathy with them.

Simmel did not think it was an accident that cities have long been the centers of a money economy. His point was not to deny the circulation of money in rural contexts or to vilify cities. It was, instead, to note that in farming and village communities there existed forms of exchange in which the personality of workers and the fruitfulness of a region could (potentially) be felt and appreciated. A barrel wasn't an anonymous product costing a certain amount. It reflected the skills of a particular cooper who could transform an oak tree that grew nearby into something useful. It (potentially) honored the tree, the skill of the cooper, and its user. By contrast, the matter-of-fact calculating mind that dominates urban centers had the effect of "transforming the world into an arithmetic problem and of fixing every one of its parts in a mathematical formula. It has been the money economy which has thus filled the daily life of so many people with weighing, calculating, enumerating and the reduction of qualitative values to quantitative terms."[13]

The erosion of sympathy brought about by a money economy moves within two kinds of abstraction. First, a focus on money means that people lose sight of the physical, fragile, entangled, flesh-and-blood world they necessarily depend upon to feed, warm, and house them and supply enjoyment. Fellow creatures are not reducible to commodities or units of production, nor is a store or warehouse a home. But with the unbridled pursuit of money the temptation is to render the world and its inhabitants abstract and endlessly manipulable and purchasable. As Robin puts it, "Money becomes more real than the concrete goods we are giving up or in quest of. Forgetting that money is 'a means to the enjoyments of and realities of life,' not an end, we abandon the reality of the present for the fiction of the future." Second, money also abstracts people, because "it removes us from the here and now and throws us to that 'spurious and decisive immortality' that lies beyond."[14] What Robin means is that by holding on to money people can rise above present uncertainty and place their hope in a future state of affairs that is bound to be better. The acquisition of money acts as a hedge against the vulnerabilities and mutual neediness of entangled, embodied life. But a hedge also prevents people from experiencing aspects of this world's mystery, vulnerability, and grace.

Since the publication of Simmel's essay, the power of the money economy to shape and orient life has grown dramatically. If in previous iterations capitalist economies centered on the production of goods and services, today's capitalism is finance-dominated: banking, insurance, and real estate are the preferred ways to grow maximum profits as quickly as possible. As corporations have succumbed to the hard discipline of optimizing and accelerating profits, the effects have been severe and are well known: company streamlining and the downsizing of workforces, the mechanization and roboticization of worker tasks, relocation of operations to regions with cheaper workforces and less regulation (especially as relating to worker and environmental protections), the hyperinflation of land and housing prices owing to speculator investment, and corporate restructuring in response to ever-changing market opportunities and demands. In a world of shrinking markets that is also awash with commodities, cutting costs is essential, and the best way to do that is to cut down the workforce and then demand more from the workers who are left.

Finance capitalism places workers in positions of inordinate stress. Amazon employees, for instance, know they are constantly being watched, their every move monitored and timed, with the result that they do not have the time to think, go to the bathroom, or socialize with co-workers. Having been reduced to performing the same tasks over and over again like machines, many sustain injuries and suffer from the mind-numbing exhaustion that is a contemporary variation of Simmel's blasé attitude. They know they are expendable, since they can readily be replaced by someone else, a robot, a delivery drone, or a driverless vehicle. Those in white collar professions are not much better off. To be successful they must show their total commitment to the company or institution; they must be prepared to sacrifice family, community, and even their own health (by constantly taking on extra work, sleeping in the office, and eating at their desk). As Kathryn Tanner has insightfully noted, "One's very person, at the level of its most fundamental projects, is to become the insertion point for company profit-taking; every employee must have an entrepreneurial self, relating to oneself as an enterprise for profit, if the company itself is to be profitable in the optimal way that finance demands."[15]

Finance capitalism also changes how people think of themselves and how they relate to others. When financial markets determine what work gets done and how, employers can say the demands they impose upon workers are not personally motivated but reflect market forces. When demands are imposed using this excuse, employers and employees lose what little sense of personal agency and responsibility they may have had. As Tanner describes it, "For all my self-initiated self-management, I am self-evacuated . . . of anything beyond which the market dictates, so that the market seems to be extending its own life in and through me." Employees also lose a reason to work in a cooperative or collegial manner, since worker performance is constantly evaluated relative to the performance of peers. Working hard isn't enough. Someone else might be working harder or get lucky. Profit maximization keeps workers in a precarious, envious condition. Everyone "is under threat from everyone else . . . gains made by co-workers can only portend one's own downfall."[16] People, Tanner says, increasingly feel that they are in winner-take-all markets and that the number of winners is steadily shrinking.

Will it shrink to zero? The now-easy use of artificial intelligence, made possible by the release of OpenAI's ChatGPT, has raised the fear that human work and creativity is doomed, not by peers or bosses, but by machines, algorithms, and the select number of investors who profit from their deployment. Teachers, lawyers, doctors, computer programmers, journalists, consultants, and artists—to name a few—are seeing that many of the tasks they once performed can now be done much more quickly, effortlessly, and cheaply by machines. They are worried about the reduction of persons to the functions they perform. They are frightened by what many see as the ultimate end of AI development: human obsolescence, if not extinction.

Finance capitalism, along with robots, chatbots, and AI systems, destroys sympathy because it makes workers anxious, frantic, and competitive—which all kill resonance. It casts a future that is volatile, undemocratic, and frightening to the many people who do not have access to streams of capital that can (temporarily) shield them. Market fluctuations, the elimination of jobs, and climate change realities threaten the stability and security of their homes. The drive for profit maximization undermines hope because it leads to the exploitation and abandonment of people and places alike.

A hopeful economy respects the life-giving relationships that join people to each other, to fellow creatures, and to their shared habitats. It honors our lives by nurturing the homes that nurture us. A hopeful community, then, is a rooted economy. The thing about roots, however, is that they do not simply extract nutrients from the soil. If they did, a growing plant would eventually deplete the soil of its fertility, and the plant would die. Roots also act as the distribution systems that transfer sunlight energy—in the form of photosynthesis-produced sugars—from its point of acquisition to below the soil surface, where it feeds a vast, often hundreds-of-miles-long, fungal meshwork of hyphae and mycelia that extends deeply into the soil in the hunt for nutrients. The more energy from sunlight that goes below-ground, feeding and extending the fungal meshwork, the more the roots and root hairs are able to support vigorous and resilient growth aboveground. Successful plant life, along with the health and vitality of all the insect and animal life that depends upon it, grows up *and* down; it hinges on the flow of nutrients going in both directions.

This image of rooted plant growth as a model for economic vitality is in stark contrast to the standard, textbook-certified model of economies as closed circular systems. The model describes the flows of money, goods, and services between firms and households. As characterized by Herman Daly, a pioneer in ecological economics, the central problem with this image is that it isn't rooted. It floats above the earth in an isolated, suspended state: "Nothing enters from the outside, nothing exits to the outside. There are no natural resources entering from the ecosphere, no wastes exiting back to the ecosphere. Indeed, there is no ecosphere, no containing and constraining environment of any kind. This abstract vision is useful for studying exchange (supply, demand, prices, and national income), but worthless for studying environmental costs of economic growth because there is no finite environment to constrain growth."[17]

Daly acknowledges that recent advocates of a "circular economy" have revised this earlier neoclassical model by advocating for the recycling of natural resources, the use of renewable energy systems, and the minimizing of waste—all good things—but the central problem remains: economic activity continues to prioritize extraction (however efficient, however clean) and fails to follow what must be the fundamental principle governing a hopeful economy: to properly nurture the natural habitats and the creaturely communities in which the economy is at work.[18]

When mutual nurture is the central economic priority,

two system-transforming commitments to places and workers come into view. First, feed the ground that feeds us. This sounds simple enough, but the history of global agriculture has most often been a history of exploitation: farmers, usually under intense pressure from financial and political elites, mine and exhaust soil fertility to grow commodities to enrich ruling classes. This system of production denudes and erodes soil, wastes and contaminates fresh water, extirpates Indigenous peoples, abuses farmworkers, and contributes to the extinction of plant, animal, and insect species.

Aidee Guzman is among a growing number of researchers who are convinced that a better form of agriculture is possible and necessary: one that nurtures the soil and the human communities that draw their food and livelihoods from it. Guzman is a soil scientist who has been tracking and studying the farmers who are cultivating biodiversity in the midst of California farms known for their production of a few staple commodities grown in dramatically simplified and degraded landscapes. She has found immigrant farmers from Mexico and Central America who are keeping alive traditions of agriculture that emphasize the cultivation of multiple species of plants. Their system (much like the "three sisters" system deployed by multiple Indigenous farmers) is called the *milpa.* It begins with the growth of corn, beans, and squash together; then peppers, tomatoes, herbs, cacti, and numerous wild plants are added to the mix. Besides producing a diverse and nutritious diet to eaters, this system also attracts insects and pollinators, confuses pests, and increases soil fertility. It has provided food security for centuries and is inspiring the farming we need in the twenty-first century.

The milpa way of farming was perfected by the Mayan people, who developed some of the most complex and diverse agricultural landscapes in the history of the world. The nearest equivalent to the word "agriculture" in the Mayan language is *MeyabjbilK'aax,* which means "working with nature." Their system of food production was steeped in a deep sympathy for the land and was based, we could say, on the idea of community: on plant, insect, and animal species working together to optimize the health and vitality of all its members. As Guzman studied the gardens of migrant farmworkers who were carrying on this ancient system, she recalled the stories her parents had told her of the farming communities in Mexico. She remembered the first trip her family made to El Pedregal to visit their ancestral home. "The moment we got there, the world opened up . . . I could see the canyon. People were harvesting. The food. My family. The animals running around. I thought it was beautiful."[19]

The landscape she encountered in El Pedregal was so unlike what she encounters now in California's Central Valley. Besides being botanically diverse, the fields made room for flowers, because they are beautiful, and trees, because they help prevent erosion. The people who lived there knew in detail the ecological, nutritional, and medicinal benefits of the plants they grew. They also saw their land as sacred, not to be taken for granted, and paused to bless it during planting season. They put the combined health of their land and their community ahead of profit maximization. Theirs was a centuries-old food economy that nourished the land and its people together. It stands in striking contrast to the industrial Green Revolution economy that, upon arriving in Mexico a few short decades ago, transformed biodiversity into a monoculture, depleted the soil, poisoned the water, and dissolved farming families and communities.

Can an agroecological way of farming play a significant, perhaps even transformative, role in today's agricultural landscape? It is hard to know. What is clear, however, is that the world's growing human population cannot feed itself from lands that are being systematically degraded and that are worked by people who are being systematically exploited.

A hopeful way ahead will depend on (increasingly urban) eaters who appreciate the importance of agroecological methods that nurture land and people alike. This is the indispensable foundation upon which current and future human flourishing depends. My recommendation is not that everyone become a farmer. It is, instead, that eaters take on the responsibility of advocating for just and healthy food systems. They can do this in multiple ways: by voting for politicians who support regenerative agriculture, who combat the absentee investors driving up land prices, and who prioritize investment in farming communities and local food systems; by purchasing food from area farmers and chefs who honor the land and its creatures; by growing even a small portion of their own fruit or vegetables; by contacting and demanding of legislators that they write food and agriculture policies that foster soil fertility and species biodiversity, that encourage food democracy, and that make nutritious food available and affordable to all eaters; and by making time to prepare, share, reflect upon, and celebrate appetizing meals with others.

Cultures have not been well served by extractive economies that mine places and then abandon them. A far better way is to cultivate places, harvest the gifts the earth provides, and then ask what an appropriate harvest requires of us. In this respect, those who live in "advanced" economies have much to learn from Indigenous communities that advocate for an "honorable harvest." As Robin Kimmerer summarizes it, this way of relating to the land requires that you:

> *Know the ways of the ones who take care of you, so that you may take care of them.*

> *Introduce yourself. Be accountable as the one who comes asking for life.*
> *Ask permission before taking. Abide by the answers.*
> *Never take the first. Never take the last.*
> *Take only what you need.*
> *Take only that which is given.*
> *Never take more than half. Leave some for others.*
> *Harvest in a way that minimizes harm.*
> *Use it respectfully. Never waste what you have taken.*
> *Share.*
> *Give thanks for what you have been given.*
> *Give a gift, in reciprocity for what you have taken.*
> *Sustain the ones who sustain you and the earth will last forever.*[20]

I recognize that the sympathies and sensibilities, let alone the practices, of the "honorable harvest" cannot simply be integrated into today's dominant economies. The modes and manners of the latter are in direct opposition to the ways of the former. Clearly, however, our fossil-fuel-driven, endlessly extractive, poison-spreading economies are leading us, quite literally, to a dead end. We need the wisdom of the "honorable harvest" as a vital standard by which to judge the propriety of our commitments and to help us imagine and implement new/old economic forms.

If the first system-transforming commitment we need to make is to the land, the second is to support the workers that keep our economies on the move. Here, too, the history of work provides far too many examples of worker coercion and exploitation. The wealth of a few has often been acquired at the expense of a great many others.

A vision for a better way is being developed in Morganton, North Carolina, not too far from where I live. Formed in 2015, The Industrial Commons (TIC) exists to improve the livelihoods of workers and to root wealth in the (natural and social) communities in which they live. Its vision statement reads: "The Industrial Commons founds and scales employee owned social and industrial cooperatives, and supports frontline workers to build a new southern working class that erases the inequities of generational poverty and builds an economy and future for all."[21] To make the vision real, TIC is:

> investing in a new textile industry that, among other strategies, recycles previously worn T-shirts to make new blankets;
> connecting companies so that workers can learn best practices from each other;
> offering multiple job and skills-training programs;
> facilitating the transfer of frontline worker insights to management and providing coaching to supervisory staff;
> operating a loan fund called Capital for the Commons that will assist locally owned and democratically governed businesses; and
> hosting walking tours of the county that highlight and celebrate the creativity of area residents.

TIC is making plans to build an Innovation Campus that will transform an old factory into a site for the sharing and incubation of ideas and skills among small-scale to medium-scale businesses, and it is redeveloping a 10-acre parcel of downtown land into a Housing Cooperative with fifty-five housing units of varying sizes, a playground, a community garden, and a shared community clubhouse that combines the features of a land trust (to keep prices affordable) and a limited equity cooperative (to give residents a modest rate of return on their investment).

The goal of TIC is to support seventy-five sustainable, innovative, and equitable businesses by 2025. It aims to connect 10,000 area workers through its industry networks, all the while holding fast to the "Triple Bottom Line" of social well-being, environmental health, and economic justice. The aim is to create a working culture and a sympathetic economy that values kindness, embraces differences in ideas and styles, and prizes honest communication, appreciative inquiry, collaboration, generosity, and courtesy. To have a good workplace workers have to trust each other, and they have to believe that all workers should participate in the decision-making processes that guide the business. The point of a business is to be profitable, but not at the expense of worker growth and flourishing.

It is tempting to dismiss TIC's vision and plan as insignificant and as too small to make a major economic impact. But what is the proper measure by which to assess "impact"? Is it jobs saved, families kept together, communities taking pride in their businesses and neighborhoods, a high quality of life, the feeling of camaraderie and shared enterprise, the resilience of a local business, and the beauty of a work environment? TIC is a witness to what some are calling the social solidarity economy, which is an economy that prioritizes the welfare of people and the planet over profits and blind growth.[22] Businesses adhering to the values framework of the social solidarity economy are growing across the world as people recognize that the business models often prescribed by major financial institutions are not only unsustainable but ecologically and socially destructive.

Another outstanding example of the social solidarity economy is practiced by the Mondragon Corporation, located in the Basque region of northern Spain. Profiled in major news outlets (like the *New York Times* and the *New Yorker* magazine), Mondragon has become a source of inspiration for many businesspeople, including the leadership team at TIC. Mondragon was founded in 1956 when the Catholic priest José Maria Arizmendiarrieta noticed a need for good employment opportunities for area residents. Commonly referred to as "the apostle of cooperation," Arizmendiarrieta joined with other community leaders to start a kerosene heater factory. This factory was to be run as a cooperative, which meant that workers shared ownership in the company and determined the shape and flow of the work. As problems emerged, workers addressed them with the creation of yet another cooperative enterprise (as when they created an internal pension plan and health care system to respond to worker needs). The key to company success was and is worker success, which is why the needs and well-being of workers are foremost priorities.

The corporation now consists of ninety-five cooperatives and employs roughly 80,000 people (76 percent of whom co-own the co-ops they work in). In the production facilities the workers make bicycles, jet engines, wind turbines, and other large industrial machines. The corporation runs several businesses, including a large grocery store chain (Eroski), a catering company, schools, fourteen research and development centers, and a consulting firm. Those who join the staff soon have the opportunity to become worker-owners, which means they have an equal vote on the many decisions made about company strategy, policy, and compensation. They know that the managing director (a near-equivalent to a CEO) will not make more than six times the salary of the lowest paid worker. There are no outside shareholders to overrule what they as stakeholders decide.

The central idea behind a co-op is that stakeholders share whatever profits are made. When times are hard, they support each other. For instance, during the global financial crisis of 2008, members of the Mondragon Corporation had almost no worker layoffs (as compared to a 26 percent unemployment rate in Spain), and during the COVID-19 pandemic worker-owners agreed to a 5 percent pay cut and the temporary reduction of working hours so that large-scale layoffs could be avoided. Workers can often make more money working elsewhere, but as one engineer put it, there is a profound psychological benefit in knowing that others are looking out for you. "I prefer to live here with a lot of people and friends than alone like a king."[23]

TIC and the Mondragon Corporation are demonstrating that the economic systems that exploit workers and communities are not inevitable or necessary. They remind us that economic enterprises are always built and sustained by people and therefore reflect the value structures and political will of particular groups of people. What makes a social solidarity economy so noteworthy and so necessary for our time is adherents' commitment to democratic processes of engagement and decision-making.[24]

Cooperative enterprises are always vulnerable to the global economic forces that function under the rule of ruthless competition. They have difficulty, for instance, matching the costs of enterprises that exploit their workers and mine the earth. Moreover, they do not tend to thrive in neoliberal societies that valorize individual success and private virtue: visitors to Mondragon from America routinely confuse a cooperative with a communist operation, whereas visitors from Mondragon to America are struck by the apparent lack of concern for justice, fairness, and equity. Because cooperative enterprises are so vulnerable, it is important to cultivate cultures of cooperation and belonging or, we might say, communities of mutual sympathy in which collaboration and care are priorities. In the presence of each other, working together, people can design the economies we need to live in hope.

Epilogue
Learning to Dance

Throughout this book I have argued that hope is born when people come together and commit to the nurture of each other and their shared places. Hope lives in the diverse forms of "love's braided dance covering the world." The braiding of lives in the joining of hands is the fundamental need of our existence. Hands reaching out, hands cradling another, hands clasping hands, hands offering comfort and support, hands protecting and building, hands nudging and releasing, hands cheering another on—gestures like these demonstrate our shared vulnerability and self-*in*sufficiency, but also our fidelity to and our desire to live for each other. When we intentionally join together, we communicate, however inchoately, our conviction that the future is worth working toward together. Hope is the power that propels people to give themselves to the care and celebration of life with fellow creatures. By contrast, isolation, abandonment, and abuse diminish life's possibilities and erode the bases for hope.

I have also assumed that it is false to speak of an individual or isolated life. People cannot stand alone, nor can they live well entirely by themselves. Life is movement with and circulation through others. Soil, fresh water, photosynthetic and digestive processes, reproductive and daily health, caring communities, traditions of language and meaning, built environments and economies—all of these elements are constitutive of our being and identity, pulsing through our bodies at every moment. Even in death the motion never stops, as microbes and processes of decomposition break down and repurpose the body for yet more life. Living never simply means us acting upon places and fellow creatures. It also, and always, means others acting upon us, in life and in death. Eating, drinking, touching, being touched, breathing, and being inspired are the daily demonstrations of this fact. To live is to be engaged, always in relation to others.[1] To engage thoughtfully we need to consider how and what to give in response to what is received.

How should we move within life's receiving/responding dynamic? What should the goals of our intertwining movement be? Are some forms of embodied engagement more beautiful or more hopeful than others? Is there such a thing as a false move?

Dance can be defined as the artistry of bodily movement or, as dancers sometimes say, as the poetry of the body. In this art form people express through their bodies what they are feeling and how they are feeling it. The American dancer and choreographer Martha Graham put it beautifully when she said dance expresses "the state of the soul's weather." Of course, we do not need to be professional dancers on a stage to communicate through our bodies—often more honestly than with words—our varying states of fear, freedom, anxiety, possibility, power, boredom, anger, compassion, empathy, sadness, and joy. Athletes, construction workers, parents, musicians, cooks, nurses, farmers, and technicians (to name a few) can exhibit artistry of movement too. Even so, dance brings into clarifying view what human bodies are capable of and what they might aspire to achieve. As Graham has noted, "I think the reason dance has held such an ageless magic for the world is that it has been the symbol of the performance of living . . . I feel that the essence of dance is the expression of mankind—the landscape of the human soul . . . It is the eternal pulse of life, the utter desire."[2] By attending to dance, then, we have an opportunity to focus on the skills people need to navigate through this world and with each other with dignity and grace, skills like attention and listening, courage and creativity, exertion and discipline, mercy and grace. Dance matters and is instructive because, among multiple possibilities, it can give embodied expression to what a healed, beautiful, and harmonious relationship with the world and with others might look like.

A dancer often starts with a clean and open stage floor, much the way a painter starts with a blank canvas or a writer with a clean sheet of paper or blank computer screen. The possibilities are endless. Our lived worlds, by contrast, are populated by structures and fellow creatures that both limit and inspire us. As we move, we regularly encounter slopes, detours, and doors; sunshine, rain, and ice; butterflies, mosquitoes, and wasps; fatigue, aches, and injuries; friends, strangers, and enemies. Though modern technologies often hold out the promise of a "friction-free" world, the reality is that most of us experience surprise, encouragement, resistance, anger, frustration, disappointment, and joy precisely because of the variety of encounters we have every day. How should we move in a beautiful but wounded and wounding world?

There isn't an easy or straightforward answer. The desire to express yourself and join with others should not be taken for granted. Far too many people find themselves in abusive contexts or in situations where they are neglected, anxious, or exhausted. If people feel afraid or sad, chances are that they will find it difficult to move, let alone give creative expression to their deepest desires. The idea that life is a dance will seem far-fetched, if not preposterous. A safer option is to minimize engagements with others and, as much as possible, stay within the walls you have built to protect yourself. It takes considerable self-assurance and courage, and the knowledge that you have the mercy and support of others in times of trouble, to move confidently into the risky places of engagement and self-expression.

Moreover, the patterns of daily life have changed significantly within modernity as people have been taught to think of themselves more as individual, autonomous, rational, self-interested choosers/shoppers and less as members of communities, depending on, contributing to, and responsible for the communities of which they are a part. People increasingly find less reason to collaborate with others as it becomes easier to shop, eat, play, work, think, entertain, build, and worship alone. As Richard Sennett has persuasively argued, "Modern society is 'de-skilling' people in practicing cooperation."[3] Of course, people still come together, sometimes in great numbers. The question is whether their coming together creates the inspiration, solicitude, nurture, and commitment that animate "love's braided dance."

The art of improvisation can be of considerable help to us if our aim is to participate in the dance and try to negotiate what is often a bruising and unpredictable world. The merit of this art is that it does not require a neat and tidy space in which to perform a pre-planned, fully choreographed set of movements. Improvisation does not mean "do whatever you want." Rather, what improvisation requires is that you be fully attentive to yourself and your place, determine what is possible and pleasing at that moment, and respond in ways that are honest and true to what you encounter. Improvisation is a form of conversation in which participants are constantly listening to each other so that whatever speech they offer does not misrepresent, disrespect, or obliterate what they have heard. In other words, to improvise well takes discipline.

An invitation to improvise is rather intimidating. What if what I have to offer is inelegant, hurtful, refused, or embarrassing? It is often easier to settle for the formulaic or the prescribed than to personalize a response. "We all want to be loved," says Nuar Alsadir. "The problem is that you're less likely to connect with others on an emotional level if you're leading with a prototype or idea, an ego communication, rather than a spontaneous impulse. When your goal is to get a certain response—which involves projecting yourself into the position of another to anticipate and meet their imagined expectations, as opposed to staying close to the source—you're bound to flop." Alsadir does not deny that people can connect at the level of words and ideas. But if your aim is a deeper and more personal connection, then it is crucial that you communicate your conviction and commitment. "If a performer's expressions feel honest, of the moment, rather than rehearsed, the audience senses 'an authentic conversation,' connects . . . If not, there's silence."[4] In other words, people want to know that in their encounters with you they are not meeting a shell or a fake.

Performing "love's braided dance" in a fake and impersonal world is difficult because authentic engagement is erotic and passionate. To improvise well, people must believe they matter and have something valuable to give, they must feel they belong, and they must know they will be forgiven when they fail or make mistakes. They need to feel the power of life moving through and around them, and then they must want to give creative expression to that power in the things that they do. It is hard for any of this to happen apart from a community that affirms life's loveliness by nurturing, encouraging, challenging, correcting, and celebrating each other.

The flip side of performing passionately is believing that others matter just as much as you do, that they should be affirmed, welcomed, forgiven, and embraced even (perhaps especially) in contexts of injury and wrongdoing. Why, after all, would you make the effort to listen attentively to, wait patiently for, and move gently with others unless you recognize their goodness and beauty—what I would characterize as their sacred worth and their never-again-to-be-repeated gracious presence? Curiosity, respect, mercy, and compassion are at the heart of a hopeful improvisational effort. So too are anger and lament as expressions of protest in the presence of another's abuse or abandonment.

Graham believed that dancers have little to express if they do not "cultivate" themselves. The unique, irreplaceable life that you are can be discovered and developed only if you exercise the curiosity and contemplation that takes you into the mystery and miracle of your own existence and into the memories of what you have suffered and learned. Dancers must be true to themselves and to their environments if they are to be "reborn to the instant." None of this can happen without reverence for small yet beautiful things, gratitude for delicate strength, and a good measure of grace: "the grace resulting from faith . . . faith in life, in love, in people, in the act of dancing."[5]

Paiter Van Yperen, a dancer and choreographer based in the Dallas–Fort Worth area of Texas, says trust is at the heart of improvisational movement.[6] First, you must trust your own body to perform a movement, and to do that you must practice again and again. Insofar as dancers feel unstable, or fear that the ground beneath will not support them, their bodies will shrink and turn in. They will not be able to extend outward because they do not believe the body's center will support their effort. Second, you must trust your partner to welcome and enhance your movement. There is always the risk that either partner will make a mistake or take a misstep, which is why mutual surrender must always be accompanied by mutual mercy and forgiveness. This, too, takes considerable practice as each dancer learns from the other the shape and timing of their bodily movements. The key is not to contaminate or undermine another's movement by trying to control it. Insofar as a dancer is committed to imposing on the partner, the possibility of creating a new thing together evaporates.

Dancers that move beautifully together have learned to listen to what each other says, both verbally and through their body language. But there is a deeper language, what Van Yperen calls "heart language," that needs to be listened to as well. This level of communication takes us to the core of a person's being, what we might describe as the center of a person's desires, fears, and convictions. None of us have perfect clarity about ourselves or others. It takes time and patience to figure out what is going on inside so we can better express a vision for life on the outside. But as we dig deeper and exercise compassion, joy manifests itself in the form of a body that moves from places of strength. A joyful body is an integrated body, a body that is attuned to its environment, a body that feels life pulsing throughout its members, reaching out to be in resonant relationship with others.

When Graham taught her dance classes, the metric by which she judged a performance was not technical perfection. Dancers can have phenomenal technique and still lack the passion and meaning that make their movements resonate. She said, "I don't demand, at the beginning, any vestige of perfection. What I long for is the eagerness to meet life, the curiosity, the wonder that you feel when you really move . . . You have to permit yourself to feel, you have to permit yourself to be vulnerable. You may not like what you see, that is not important. You don't always have to judge." The most important thing,

Graham believed, is to cultivate in dancers the "excitement of living."[7] Or as Van Yperen says, the crucial thing is to enter your space and see it as a place of possibility and new creation, a place that because of your movement reveals potential that has not been realized before. When that happens, a future emerges that is worthy of your best efforts. Pain and frustration will make their appearances in this future, but so too will beauty and love.

The hope that emerges and grows in "love's braided dance" is our most worthy hope. But it is a hope that is without perfection; a hope born of excitement for life's goodness and beauty; a hope tied to the nurture, protection, and celebration of each other; a hope committed to mercy and forgiveness; a hope manifest in the construction of built environments and just economies that honor the lives that move within and through them; a hope witnessed in the creative gestures that resonate within the world's symphony of life.

Notes

Introduction

Epigraph: Quoted from the New Revised Standard Version. Copyright © 1989 National Council of Churches of Christ in the United States of America. Used by permission. All rights reserved worldwide. All quotations from the Bible are from this version.

1. My retelling of Carmine Menna's story is based on Emma Jane Kirby's remarkable chronicle *The Optician of Lampedusa* (London: Penguin Books, 2016). The quoted statements are Kirby's, but they are based on conversation with Carmine and have been approved by him.

2. Ibid., 1–2, 47.

3. In *The Naked Don't Fear the Water* (London: Fitzcarraldo Editions, 2022), Matthieu Aikins provides an intimate account of the struggles many migrants face. His book is based on the journey he undertook with his Afghani friend Omar, a journey that went from Afghanistan, through Turkey, on to the Greek island of Lesbos, and then, eventually, north into Germany. He describes the Mediterranean as the border that acts like a protective moat, shielding the West's wealthy citizens from the poverty "advanced" economies create and depend upon.

4. Kirby, *The Optician of Lampedusa*, 56.

5. Ibid., 109.

6. See the *Global Trends: Forced Displacement in 2022* report by the UNHCR at https://www.unhcr.org/global-trends-report-2022.

7. Aikins, *The Naked Don't Fear the Water*, 154.

8. In *The Will to See: Dispatches from a World of Misery and Hope* (New Haven: Yale University Press, 2021), Bernard-Henri Lévy describes camp Moria on the Greek island of Lesbos. Lesbos is one of Greece's most beautiful and lush islands, but it has become "Europe's capital of pain" because it "houses"

thousands of migrants seeking a home in Europe. The original camp was designed to hold 800 soldiers, then was redesigned to house 3,000 refugees, but now holds 20,000. It lacks running water and latrines. People are required to make do with one liter (a little less than a quart) of water per day to drink, cook, bathe, do their laundry, and disinfect. If there is space between tents, families dig holes in the ground for their excrement to avoid the public facilities, which offer no privacy and are spattered with excrement, infested with flies, and suffused with a fetid odor. Everywhere people are standing in lines, waiting, wanting, but rarely receiving anything of value at all. "Humiliation, Torture. As the rest of Europe is obsessing over public health and hygiene and how often we wash our hands, Moria is beset with infection, corruption, and stench, with little water to be found. *Anus mundi*" (150).

9. Patrick Chamoiseau, *Migrant Brothers: A Poet's Declaration of Human Dignity* (New Haven: Yale University Press, 2018), xiv. Chamoiseau describes the terrain of migrants as "lawless spaces" in which "human beings become strangers to humanity . . . Around them, those who come as humans toward other humans, whose only crime is to be human and call out to their brothers and sisters from the depths of a very human distress, find themselves faced with systems that no longer know how to recognize a human being" (ibid.).

10. See Jon Henley, "Climate Crisis Could Displace 1.2bn People by 2050, Report Warns," *Guardian*, September 9, 2020, https://www.theguardian.com/environment/2020/sep/09/climate-crisis-could-displace-12bn-people-by-2050-report-warns.

11. Disappointment in the failures of individuals and communities to provide the love that nourishes hope is often used to argue that humanity's "true" hope lies in God. So much depends, however, on what people believe about God. A capricious and inscrutable God—no matter how powerful—can hardly be the basis of our hope, since this God can just as well, and without reason, damn or save us. The God who "is love" (1 John 4:8), however, and is made known in Jesus's ministries of feeding, healing, and reconciling, and in the hospitable and caring ways of his beloved community, inspires genuine hope because this God is committed to everyone's well-being. The question of practical significance is whether this divine love is being realized in this world. It would be cruel to withhold compassion and care while asking people to put their hope in an inscrutable God.

12. In *Winter Notes on Summer Impressions* (Evanston, IL: Northwestern University Press, 1988), Fyodor Dostoevsky wondered what it would take, in the wake of the French Revolution's idealization of *liberté, égalité,* and *fraternité,* for something like the brotherhood of humanity to be realized. He observed that "Western man speaks of brotherhood as the great motivating

force of mankind and does not realize that nowhere is brotherhood achieved if it does not exist in reality. What is to be done? Brotherhood must be created no matter what. But it turns out that brotherhood cannot be created because it creates itself, is given and found in nature. But in the French nature—to be sure, in the Western nature in general—it has not shown up; what has shown up is a principle of individuality, a principle of isolation, of urgent self-preservation, self-interest, and self-determination for one's own *I*" (48). Brotherhood, like hope, depends on a transformed personality and a transformed culture in which people spontaneously seek the good of others. The idea of brotherhood needs to "enter into the flesh and blood in order to become a reality" (49). Dostoevsky did not believe the entrance of brotherly love into the world happens easily. It can take generations for it to become a cultural force. People learn it by seeing it and by practicing loving ways of being.

13. Wendell Berry, "In Rain," in *Collected Poems, 1957–1982* (San Francisco: North Point Press, 1984), 268.

14. Wendell Berry, "Discipline and Hope," in *A Continuous Harmony: Essays Cultural and Agricultural* (New York: Harcourt Brace Jovanovich, 1972), 131.

15. In *Radical Hope: Ethics in the Face of Cultural Devastation* (Cambridge, MA: Harvard University Press, 2006), Jonathan Lear says that what makes hope radical is "that it is directed toward a future goodness that transcends the current ability to understand what it is. Radical hope anticipates a good for which those who have the hope as yet lack the appropriate concepts with which to understand it" (103).

16. In *Hope without Optimism* (Charlottesville: University of Virginia Press, 2015), Terry Eagleton says, "Optimists are conservatives because their faith in a benign future is rooted in their trust in the essential soundness of the present. Indeed, optimism is a typical component of ruling-class ideologies . . . Only if you view your situation as critical do you recognize the need to transform it. Dissatisfaction can be a goad to reform . . . True hope is needed most when the situation is at its starkest, a state of extremity that optimism is generally loath to acknowledge" (4–5).

1
Erotic Hope

1. In a conversation with Britt Wray, Kyle Whyte contrasts the hope that is committed to action with the hope that waits for a miracle. The latter is often disingenuous and dangerous because the political and economic structures that perpetuate current forms of privilege also make a miracle even more

improbable. See interview with Kyle Whyte, "How Can You Hope When You Are Coming Out of a Dystopia?" *Gen Dread,* October 16, 2020, https://gendread.substack.com/p/how-can-you-hope-when-youre-coming.

2. Both quotations are from a conversation between Greta Thunberg and Alexandra Ocasio-Cortez published by the *Guardian,* June 29, 2019, as "When Alexandria Ocasio-Cortez Met Greta Thunberg: 'Hope Is Contagious,'" https://www.theguardian.com/environment/2019/jun/29/alexandria-ocasio-cortez-met-greta-thunberg-hope-contagious-climate.

3. Rebecca Solnit, *Hope in the Dark: Untold Histories, Wild Possibilities* (Chicago: Haymarket Books, 2016), 4.

4. Rebecca Solnit and Thelma Young Lutunatabua, *Not Too Late: Changing the Climate Story from Despair to Possibility* (Chicago: Haymarket Books, 2023), 192.

5. Audre Lorde, "Uses of the Erotic: The Erotic as Power," in *Sister Outsider: Essays and Speeches* (Trumansburg, NY: Crossing Press, 1984), 54.

6. Ibid., 57.

7. I recognize that the Greek term for love in this 1 Corinthians passage is *agape* rather than *eros.* These two forms—along with other Greek terms for love, like *philia, mania, ludus, storge,* and *philautia*—differ from each other (*agape* is often characterized as more self-less than *eros,* which is often characterized as acquisitive). But as I make clear in this chapter, *agape* need not stand in opposition to *eros.* Rather, *agape* complements and refines *eros.* We could even argue that the creation of the world "from nothing" (*ex nihilo,* as theologians came to describe it) is best understood as the creation of the world "from nothing but love" (*ex amore*) because love is the material expression of a divine eroticism in which God gives Godself to the creation and care of every person and every creature. Being the source of all goodness and beauty, God did not need to create anything at all. The existence of creatures, therefore, is a testament to the erotic movement in which God's goodness and beauty "overflow" and, in this outbound, overflowing movement, establish, sustain, and delight in life. Christians believe this way of speaking is warranted because Jesus embodies this movement in his ministries of feeding, friendship, healing, and forgiveness.

8. I am grateful to Lisa Eddy, Mark's wife, for granting me permission to tell Mark's story.

9. James Baldwin, *The Fire Next Time,* in *Collected Essays,* ed. Toni Morrison (New York: Library of America, 1998), 309–10.

10. Ibid., 311, 314.

11. James Baldwin, "Nothing Personal," in *The Price of the Ticket: Collected Nonfiction, 1948–1985* (Boston: Beacon Press, 1985), 391.

12. Ibid., 393.

13. In *Begin Again: James Baldwin's America and Its Urgent Lessons for Our Own* (New York: Crown, 2020), Eddie S. Glaude Jr. says, "The white southerner had to lie *continuously* to himself in order to justify his world. Lie that the black people around him were inferior. Lie about what he was doing under the cover of night. Lie that he was a Christian" (49).

14. James Baldwin, "To Crush a Serpent," in *The Cross of Redemption: Uncollected Writings*, ed. Randall Kenan (New York: Pantheon Books, 2010), 197.

15. Baldwin, "Nothing Personal," 400.

2
When Hope Languishes

1. Tony Judt, *Postwar: A History of Europe since 1945* (New York: Penguin Books, 2005), 20. The brutality of the Red Army was well known, as was Joseph Stalin's endorsement of pillage and rape. In a conversation with Milovan Djilas, a fervent communist at the time and a close collaborator with Josip Tito, Stalin asked Djilas if he couldn't understand a soldier "who has gone through blood and fire and death, if he has fun with a woman or takes a trifle" (ibid.).

2. Quoted in ibid., 19.

3. Quoted by Anne O'Hare McCormick in "The Shrouded Future of the Battlefield Once Europe," *New York Times*, March 14, 1945, p. 18, https://timesmachine.nytimes.com/timesmachine/1945/03/14/88205452.html?pageNumber=18. Eisenhower's declaration, but even more his tactics, demonstrate that the widely held belief that Allied forces were the "good guys," bringing liberation and light to a dark continent, needs to be revised. The historian Keith Lowe writes, "The men the Americans now call 'the Greatest Generation' were not all the selfless heroes they are often portrayed to be: a proportion of them were also thieves, plunderers and abusers of the worst kind" (*Savage Continent: Europe in the Aftermath of World War II* [New York: St. Martin's, 2012], 57). Some Allied commanders did not hesitate at the thought of the outright extermination of Germans through bombing and starvation. Among the many disturbing policies that have recently come to light is the inhumane treatment of German prisoners, many of them adolescent boys, in camps set up by French and American forces. These "camps" were open fields with no shelter of any kind. Young men resorted to digging holes in the ground to find relief from inclement weather. There was no food or water. Disease was rampant. My uncle Emil, my father's older brother, was in one of these camps. He told me once that when a tanker truck carrying water came through the gates, the water was dumped on the ground. Men and boys scrambled and jostled to slurp whatever water they could extract

from the mud. James Bacque was among the first historians to bring to light the long-concealed military archives that chronicle the existence of and conditions in these camps. He notes: "It is beyond doubt that enormous numbers of men of all ages, plus some women and children, died of exposure, unsanitary conditions, disease and starvation in the American and French camps in Germany and France starting in April 1945, just before the end of the war in Europe. The victims undoubtedly number over 800,000, almost certainly over 900,000 and quite likely over a million. Their deaths were knowingly caused by army officers who had sufficient resources to keep the prisoners alive. Relief organizations that attempted to help the prisoners in American camps were refused permission by the army. All of this was hidden at the time, then lied about when the Red Cross, *Le Monde* and *Le Figaro* attempted to tell the truth publicly" (*Other Losses: An Investigation into the Mass Deaths of German Prisoners at the Hands of the French and Americans after World War II* [Toronto: Stoddard, 1989], 2). More recently, R. M. Douglas has given a fuller picture of this aspect of the war's aftermath in *Orderly and Humane: The Expulsion of the Germans after the Second World War* (New Haven: Yale University Press, 2012), arguing that this history of expulsions is "one from which few if any of those directly involved emerge in a creditable light" (3). My aim in raising this complex history is not to exonerate Germans or to paint all American military officials as villains (my grandfather Wilhelm often told me that the commander at the prisoner-of-war camp in Fort Benning treated the German soldiers with respect, even with care and compassion). It is, instead, to emphasize that few people are immune to the moral and psychic ravages that war precipitates.

4. McCormick, "The Shrouded Future of the Battlefield Once Europe," 18.

5. In *Lost Witnesses: An Oral History of the Children of World War II* (New York: Random House, 2019), Svetlana Alexievich gives us a powerful glimpse of what children were feeling and thinking during the war and its aftermath. Several consistent themes emerge: a longing for a safe home; a desire to be held by one's parents; incredulity in the face of senseless destruction ("Why are they bombing cemeteries?"); constant, mind-numbing hunger; constant fear; and a longing to experience goodness and love. Marina Karyanova spoke for many children when she said, "I wanted to eat all the time. But still more I wanted someone to hug me, caress me. There was little tenderness then, there was war all around, everybody was in grief" (69).

6. Quoted in Lowe, *Savage Continent*, 1. Lowe does a particularly good job of highlighting the moral and spiritual devastation that Europeans suffered.

7. Jürgen Osterhammel, *The Transformation of the World: A Global History of the Nineteenth Century*, trans. Patrick Camiller (Princeton, NJ: Princeton University Press, 2014), 171. It is difficult to overestimate the importance of

sanitation, hygiene, and innovations in medicine in extending the life expectancy of countless people.

8. Robert Pogue Harrison, *Juvenescence: A Cultural History of Our Age* (Chicago: University of Chicago Press, 2016), 127.

9. Matthew Schneider-Mayerson and Leong Kit Ling, "Eco-Reproductive Concerns in the Age of Climate Change," *Climatic Change* 163 (2020): 1007–1023, https://link.springer.com/article/10.1007%2Fs10584-020-02923-y).

10. The results of the survey are available in Elizabeth Marks and Caroline Hickman, et al., "Climate Anxiety in Children and Young People and Their Beliefs about Government Responses to Climate Change: A Global Survey," *The Lancet Planetary Health* 5:12, December 2021, https://www.sciencedirect.com/science/article/pii/S2542519621002783?ssrnid=3918955&dgcid=SSRN_redirect_SD.

11. "The Climate Crisis Is a Child Rights Crisis: Introducing the Children's Climate Risk Index," UNICEF, August 19, 2021, https://data.unicef.org/resources/childrens-climate-risk-index-report/.

12. Greta Thunberg, *No One Is Too Small to Make a Difference* (New York: Penguin, 2018), 106.

13. Intergovernmental Panel on Climate Change, *Climate Change 2023: Synthesis Report* (Geneva, Switzerland: IPCC, 2023). The report is available at https://www.ipcc.ch/report/ar6/syr/.

14. Thunberg, *No One Is Too Small to Make a Difference,* 22.

3
Resonant Hope

1. Anna Wiener, *Uncanny Valley: A Memoir* (New York: Farrar, Straus and Giroux, 2020), 39, 3–4.

2. Ibid., 144, 136. Wiener recalls listening to the CEO of her company marketing an e-reading app at a staff meeting. "As he continued his pitch, it became clear to me that the utility of the e-reading app was not so much about reading as it was about signaling you were the type of person who *would* read, and would use an app with a cutting edge reading experience and innovative, intuitive design" (20). The aim of the app was not to enhance reading itself but to promote a lifestyle and a persona. Books, in other words, were an opportunity to grow app subscriptions rather than literacy.

3. Ibid., 186, 187.

4. Malcolm Harris, *Palo Alto: A History of California, Capitalism, and the World* (New York: Little, Brown, 2023), 79.

5. Ibid., 564.

6. "If bionomics was the theory, eugenics was the practice. Progressive

breeding was the basis for the Palo Alto system . . . and under Jordan, the small, young university became a national center for controlled evolution. He was the inaugural chair of the Committee on Eugenics at the American Breeders' Association in 1906 and served as a vice president of the First International Eugenics Congress, in London, six years later . . . Budding geniuses needed to be identified and elevated, while young degenerates needed to be corralled where they couldn't dilute the national race or turn their underachievement into social problems. In the first half of the twentieth century, Stanford made large contributions to both strategies, promoting inequality as the only policy compatible with nature" (ibid., 102, 105).

7. Ibid., 568. "Competition and domination, exploitation and exclusion, minority rule and class hate: These aren't problems capitalist technology will solve. *That's what it is for.* In the proper language, they are features, not bugs" (606).

8. Ibid., 566. The idea that people are "lifeless bodies in a system" aligns neatly with the transhumanist view that people are basically machines and their minds computational processes. Transhumanism is the signature philosophy of Palo Alto.

9. Luke Fernandez and Susan J. Matt, *Bored, Lonely, Angry, Stupid: Changing Feelings about Technology, from the Telegraph to Twitter* (Cambridge, MA: Harvard University Press, 2019), 4, 20.

10. Ibid., 139.

11. Hartmut Rosa, *Resonance: A Sociology of Our Relationship to the World* (Cambridge, UK: Polity Press, 2019), 169. In *Sources of the Self: The Making of the Modern Identity* (Cambridge, MA: Harvard University Press, 1989), Charles Taylor argues that the modern scientific, technological enterprise has had the effect of eroding, if not eliminating, the moral valence of things and places. Here, "is" and "ought" are firmly separated. By contrast, Rosa argues that "in moments of resonance 'what is' and 'what ought to be' tend to coincide" (170).

12. In *The Stars in Our Pockets: Getting Lost and Sometimes Found in the Digital Age* (Boston: Beacon Press, 2020), Howard Axelrod says, "Empathy is inefficient and slow. Empathy is unwieldy and unpredictable. It doesn't fit in the schedule. It happens in a kitchen late at night . . . nearly always involves the body, whether a glance, or a hand on the arm, or maybe a full snot-running hug . . . a return to tenderness and fragility and a nonphysical kind of strength . . . Empathy also requires humility" (141).

13. The philosopher Byung-Chul Han makes the helpful distinction between a disciplinary and an achievement paradigm. Under the former, workers encounter limits to what they should and should not do, but under the latter, workers have no limits. Limits (like defined vacation periods, overtime hours, time for travel to and from work) are removed under the achievement

paradigm. Given "unlimited" vacation days, elimination of overtime, and wi-fi-equipped transportation service, workers are encouraged to do all that they can all the time. "To heighten productivity, the paradigm of disciplination is replaced by the paradigm of achievement, or, in other words, by the positive scheme of Can . . . The positivity of Can is much more efficient than the negativity of Should. Therefore, the social unconscious switches from Should to Can. The achievement-subject is faster and more productive than the obedience-subject" (*The Burnout Society* [Redwood, CA: Stanford University Press, 2015], 9). Theoretically, there is no limit to what a worker "can" do and thus no point at which a worker has done enough.

14. Hartmut Rosa, *The Uncontrollability of the World* (Cambridge, UK: Polity Press, 2020), 44.

15. Axelrod argues that Google's product Wonder is actually an anti-wonder product: "Real wonder tends to come, even for adults, when the unknowable flashes through the known—the mystery of our place in the universe made tangible in a meteor shower, or a sudden silence in the trees that seems to let us in, or even in a grasshopper. But Google makes everything appear fully knowable, indeed already fully known, so all we need to do is reference and cross-reference intelligently and efficiently . . . Wonder is in your hands! Wonder isn't a potent swirl of curiosity and awe. Wonder doesn't take time, or have anything to do with the unknowable, or grace you with the humility to kneel down in the grass. Wonder is control" (*The Stars in Our Pockets,* 64).

16. Rosa, *The Uncontrollability of the World,* 116.

17. In my book *This Sacred Life: Humanity's Place in a Wounded World* (New York: Cambridge University Press, 2021), I explain why it is a mistake to think that God creates and relates to the world in the modalities of control and domination.

18. It is important to underscore that Israel's sabbath teaching had important, and from a historical point of view, revolutionary economic and social/political dimensions affecting the treatment of people, fellow creatures, and the land itself. I explore the practical difference sabbath teaching makes in my book *Living the Sabbath: Discovering the Rhythms of Rest and Delight* (Grand Rapids, MI: Brazos Press, 2006).

4
Hope Grows in Places of Belonging

1. Henry David Thoreau, *The Journal, 1837–1861,* ed. Damion Searls (New York: New York Review of Books, 2009), 90–91. Thoreau's regret about his body's failure to function like a musical instrument is part of what he took to

be an overall failure to train our senses to fully encounter the world around. In his book *A Week on the Concord and Merrimack Rivers,* published in 1849 but about a roughly two-week journey that happened in 1839, Thoreau said, "Our present senses are but the rudiments of what they are destined to become. We are comparatively deaf and dumb and blind, and without smell or taste or feeling . . . The eyes were not made for such groveling uses as they are now put to and worn out by, but to behold beauty now invisible" (*A Week on the Concord and Merrimack Rivers* [Princeton, NJ: Princeton University Press, 1980], 382).

2. Robin Wall Kimmerer, *Braiding Sweetgrass: Indigenous Wisdom, Scientific Knowledge and the Teachings of Plants* (Minneapolis: Milkweed Editions, 2015), 124–25.

3. Ibid., 126.

4. Ibid., 126–27.

5. Sue Stuart-Smith. *The Well-Gardened Mind: The Restorative Power of Nature* (New York: Scribner, 2020), 288.

6. Ibid., 66.

7. Ibid., 85.

8. Ibid., 172.

5
A Forgiveness-Seeking Hope

1. Recordings of their song can be heard at the Cornell Lab's All About Birds website, at https://www.allaboutbirds.org/guide/Western_Meadowlark/sounds#.

2. I am grateful to Don and Marie Ruzicka for sharing their story with me and for helping me understand its importance.

3. In the nineteenth century the Canadian government signed multiple treaties with First Nations peoples. These treaties were designed to further the land settlement aims of the government, most notably for natural resource and agricultural development. Besides removing Indigenous peoples from their lands (and relocating them to reservations), these treaties also precipitated the end of Indigenous ways of life. In return for land, the government promised food and medicine, but its promises were rarely fully kept, which is why multiple tribes refused or were reluctant to sign the treaties. The workaround was simple: "If a tribe or a band refused to sign a removal treaty, government officials would find a few members who could be convinced to sign, and then the treaty would be applied to the whole tribe. Native people opposed to such treaties and tactics were frequently threatened with military action. Annuity payments from a previous treaty would be withheld to force

compliance. A food source such as the buffalo would be driven off or destroyed in order to bring Indians to heel. These were some of the methods used . . . to force Big Bear's Cree to sign Treaty Six in 1876" (Thomas King, *The Inconvenient Indian: A Curious Account of Native People in North America* [Toronto: Doubleday Canada, 2012], 87).

4. This new push did not arise in a historical vacuum. It was preceded and informed by decades of economic and political policies that prepared the way for industrial agricultural development. Not the least of the policies was the removal of First Nations people from their ancestral lands. Jim Selby observes: "Beginning in 1897, the pace of westward migration had accelerated. Lured by the promise of free homesteads, the rising international price of wheat, and government propaganda, tens of thousands of would-be farmers from central and eastern Canada and from Europe moved to the Canadian prairies" ("One Step Forward: Alberta Workers, 1885–1914," in *Working People in Alberta: A History*, ed. Alvin Finkel [Edmonton: Athabasca University Press, 2014], 71). In the following decades, volatile grain prices, unfavorable weather, and increasing mechanization led to ever-larger farms controlled by a smaller number of people, while ever-smaller profit margins for farmers necessitated maximization of yield. Smaller profit margins for farmers also went hand in hand with increased costs for machinery and farm inputs like fertilizers and herbicides.

5. Desmond M. Tutu and Mpho A. Tutu, *The Book of Forgiving: The Fourfold Path for Healing Ourselves and Our World* (London: William Collins, 2014), 166.

6. Matthew Ichihashi Potts, *Forgiveness: An Alternative Account* (New Haven: Yale University Press, 2022), 10. Potts insists that it is a mistake to think that forgiveness always provides a happy ending. "It is not a simple resolution to conflict because the legacies of harm are long-standing and not easily eradicable" (182).

7. Tutu and Tutu, *The Book of Forgiving*, 165.

8. Ibid., 180.

9. The text of the pope's address can be found here: "'I Am Deeply Sorry': Full Text of Residential School Apology from Pope Francis," *Canadian Press*, posted July 25, 2022, https://www.cbc.ca/news/canada/edmonton/pope-francis-maskwacis-apology-full-text-1.6531341.

10. Pope Francis, "'I Am Deeply Sorry.'" In his address Francis quotes Eli Wiesel, who says "the opposite of love is not hatred, it's indifference, and the opposite of life is not death, it's indifference."

11. Since the pope's trip to Alberta, the Vatican has worked to clarify its position vis-à-vis the "Doctrine of Discovery." In the March 30, 2023, "Joint Statement of the Dicasteries for Culture and Education and for Promoting

Integral Human Development on the 'Doctrine of Discovery,'" the Office of the Holy See acknowledged that Christians have committed evil acts against Indigenous peoples. But as Pope Francis has emphasized, the sufferings of Indigenous peoples "constitute a powerful summons to abandon the colonizing mentality and to walk humbly with them side by side, in mutual respect and dialogue, recognizing the rights and cultural values of all individuals and peoples." The Joint Statement goes on to say that the legal concept of "discovery" was debated by colonial powers from the sixteenth century on, and some legal scholars at the time made appeals to the papal bulls *Dum Diversas* (1452), *Romanus Pontifex* (1455), and *Inter Caetera* (1493) as justification to take full possession of Indigenous lands. Even so, according to the Joint Statement, "the 'doctrine of discovery' is not part of the teaching of the Catholic Church. Historical research clearly demonstrates that the papal documents . . . have never been considered expressions of the Catholic faith. At the same time, the Church acknowledges that these papal bulls did not adequately reflect the equal dignity and rights of indigenous peoples." The statement asserts further that the Holy See gives strong support for the principles of the UN Declaration on the Rights of Indigenous Peoples. "In no uncertain terms, the Church's magisterium upholds the respect due to every human being. The Catholic Church therefore repudiates those concepts that fail to recognize the inherent human rights of indigenous peoples, including what has become known as the legal and political 'doctrine of discovery.'" (For the full text see Joint Statement of the Dicasteries for Culture and Education and for Promoting Integral Human Development on the "Doctrine of Discovery," 30.03.2023, Holy See Press Office, https://press.vatican.va/content/salastampa/en/bollettino/pubblico/2023/03/30/230330b.html.)

12. The Indigenous writer Linda Hogan says it this way: "We want a healing, I think, a cure for anguish, a remedy that will heal the wound between us and the world that contains our broken histories" (*Dwellings: A Spiritual History of the World* [New York: Norton, 1995], 76).

13. The story of the Tanderups is told by Margaret Jacobs in *After One Hundred Winters* (Princeton, NJ: Princeton University Press, 2021), 12–13. For further resources on reconciliation efforts see the website Reconciliation Rising: Confronting Our Past, Reimagining Our Future, https://www.reconciliationrising.org.

6
A Forgiveness-Granting Hope

1. Cynthia Ngewu's story and testimony are told in Antjie Krog's two powerful accounts of South Africa's Truth and Reconciliation Commission,

Country of My Skull: Guilt, Sorrow, and the Limits of Forgiveness in the New South Africa (New York: Three Rivers Press, 1999) and *Conditional Tense: Memory and Vocabulary after the South African Truth and Reconciliation Commission* (London: Seagull Books, 2013), 41–42. Krog received the Pringle Award for excellence in journalism for her reporting on the TRC's proceedings.

2. Pumla Gobodo-Madikizela's *A Human Being Died That Night: A South African Woman Confronts the Legacy of Apartheid* (New York: Houghton Mifflin, 2003), 14–15.

3. Nelson Mandela, "People Are Destroyed," in *No Easy Walk to Freedom: Speeches, Letters, and Other Writings,* ed. Ato Quayson (London: Penguin Books, 2002), 24. Mandela is clear that the policies of the South African government were continuing the stated objective of Cecil Rhodes, which was to ensure a cheap labor force for industry. Mandela's formulation: "What is wanted by the ruling circles is a docile, spineless, unorganized, and inarticulate army of workers" ("Land Hunger," in *No Easy Walk to Freedom,* 27).

4. Nelson Mandela, *Long Walk to Freedom: The Autobiography of Nelson Mandela* (New York: Little, Brown, 1994), 539.

5. Ibid., 568.

6. Ibid., 617. When de Klerk and Mandela were jointly awarded the Nobel Peace Prize in 1993, Mandela spoke of de Klerk in his acceptance speech: "He had the courage to admit that a terrible wrong had been done to our country and people through the imposition of the system of apartheid. He had the foresight to understand and accept that all the people of South Africa must, through negotiations and as equal participants in the process, together determine what they want to make of their future" (612). Mandela's words did not erase or weaken his severe criticisms of de Klerk and his government. What was important, however, is that he did not work to undermine de Klerk or try to make him weak, since that would have undermined the negotiation process too. The future of South Africa required that they work together as partners.

7. Krog, *Conditional Tense,* 35, 83. Across Africa a diversity of cultures express ubuntu teaching in their own ways. In the Zulu idiom, for instance, the phrase translates as "a person is a person through other persons" (51). Krog's preferred definition is "interconnectedness-towards-wholeness": "It means both a mental and physical awareness that one can only 'become' who one is, or could be, through the fullness of that which is round one—both physical and metaphysical. Wholeness is thus not a passive state or nirvana but a process of becoming in which everyone and everything moves toward its fullest self, building itself. One can, however, only reach that fullest self through and with others, which includes ancestors and the universe" (196).

8. Ibid., 51, 84. Krog concluded: "Indeed, in many ways the whole no-

tion of separateness, apartness and, finally, apartheid is the absolute antithesis of what communalism and interconnectedness was all about" (52).

9. Tutu saw in Mandela the embodiment of the forgiveness required of ubuntu teaching. Mandela, in his autobiography, wrote, "I knew as well as I knew anything that the oppressor must be liberated just as surely as the oppressed. A man who takes away another man's freedom is a prisoner of hatred, he is locked behind the bars of prejudice and narrow-mindedness. I am not truly free if I am taking away someone else's freedom, just as surely as I am not free when my freedom is taken from me. The oppressed and the oppressor alike are robbed of their humanity . . . to be free is not merely to cast off one's chains, but to live in a way that respects and enhances the freedom of others" (*Long Walk to Freedom,* 624–25).

10. Desmond Mpilo Tutu, *No Future without Forgiveness* (New York: Doubleday, 1999), 273.

11. In *The Book of Forgiving; The Fourfold Path for Healing Ourselves and Our World* (London: William Collins, 2014), Desmond M. Tutu and Mpho A. Tutu describe two aspects to this courage. First, "The only way to experience healing and peace is to forgive. Until we can forgive, we remain locked in our pain and locked out of the possibility of experiencing healing and freedom . . . Until we can forgive the person who harmed us, that person will hold the keys to our happiness, that person will be our jailor. When we forgive, we take back control of our own fate and feelings. We become our own liberators" (16). And second, "It is a remarkable feat to be able to see past the inhumanity of the behavior and recognize the humanity of the person committing the atrocious acts. This is not weakness. This is heroic strength, the noblest strength of the human spirit" (34).

12. Pumla Gobodo-Madikizela, "Intersubjectivity and Embodiment: Exploring the Role of the Maternal in the Language of Forgiveness and Reconciliation," *Signs: Journal of Women in Culture and Society* 36, no. 3 (2011): 546 (commas added).

13. Ibid., 547, 550.

14. Gobodo-Madikizela comes to this insight by engaging the Jewish philosopher Emmanuel Levinas, who argued that responsibility for another requires that we bear him or her "like a maternal body." Speaking of the vulnerability implied in our relationships with other people, Levinas says maternity is "gestation of the other . . . In maternity what signifies is a responsibility for others, to the point of substitution for others" (*Otherwise Than Being, or Beyond Essence,* trans. Alphonso Lingis [The Hague: Martinus Nijhoff, 1981], 75). Gobodo-Madikizela concludes that by locating "the essence of our ethical responsibility in the heart of the body, as symbolized by the maternal body, Levinas's ethical observations call us to respond to the traumatic dis-

ruption of the past not with the moral force of righteous aggression but with the moral force of love, as we would to the child from our womb. In this context, the image of *inimba* is an evocative one because it draws us to respond to the suffering of the Other as if the Other were the child that one carried in one's womb" ("Intersubjectivity and Embodiment," 550).

15. Tutu and Tutu, *The Book of Forgiving*, 22.

16. Gobodo-Madikizela, *A Human Being Died That Night*, 32.

17. Ibid., 34.

18. Tutu stated again and again that sympathy for others depends on an affirmation of the fundamental goodness of people and the realization that this goodness can be denied or distorted in any one of us. Individuals are susceptible to doing horrific things—often as the result of being bruised and broken by others—but the moment they are deemed to be essentially evil, all hope for them is lost. This is why the Tutus say, "There is nothing that cannot be forgiven, and there is no one undeserving of forgiveness" (*The Book of Forgiving*, 3). Tutu believed that all people are created and loved by God and that there is nothing a person can do that will make God stop loving anyone. "Our nature is goodness. Yes, we do much that is bad, but our essential nature is good. If it were not, then we would not be shocked and dismayed when we harm one another" (6). Mandela shared Tutu's affirmation of humanity's fundamental goodness. He argued that brutalizing behavior was the effect of a brutalizing environment that taught and rewarded it. "I always knew that deep down in every human heart, there is mercy and generosity. No one is born hating another person because of the color of his skin, or his background, or his religion. People must learn to hate, and if they can learn to hate, they can be taught to love, for love comes more naturally to the human heart than its opposite. Even in the grimmest times in prison, when my comrades and I were pushed to our limits, I would see a glimmer of humanity in one of the guards, perhaps just for a second, but it was enough to reassure me and keep me going. Man's goodness is a flame that can be hidden but never extinguished" (*Long Walk to Freedom*, 622).

19. Gobodo-Madikizela, *A Human Being Died That Night*, 99.

20. Quoted in Jacqueline Rose, "One Long Scream—Trauma and Justice in South Africa," in *On Violence and On Violence against Women* (New York: Farrar, Straus and Giroux, 2021), 307.

21. Tutu, *No Future without Forgiveness*, 279; Desmond Tutu, *God Has a Dream: A Vision of Hope for Our Times* (London: Ebury Digital, 2011), 55–56.

22. Krog observes that Afrikaners disavowed their violent past and therefore lived in a condition of trauma and shame. "One could say that the trauma suffered during the Anglo-Boer War has been transmitted perfectly on to the next generations but what has been denied/disavowed is the parents' perpe-

tration of violence through and during apartheid. Afrikaners have failed to find a structure which could navigate their movement from the honorable Anglo-Boer War past through the shameful apartheid past into a new identity within the new South Africa" (*Conditional Tense,* 186). In *Begin Again: James Baldwin's America and Its Urgent Lesson for Our Own* (New York: Crown, 2020), Eddie S. Glaude Jr. describes in detail the similar inability of many Americans to call America's past violent and racist and then navigate a way into a just and hopeful future.

23. Rose, "Afterword," in *On Violence and On Violence against Women,* 363. Rose builds upon Sigmund Freud's concept of "derealization," which describes the complex, often subterranean, processes whereby a person goes to great lengths to "avoid what it cannot bear to know about itself" (205). From a psychoanalytic perspective, however, nothing perishes in the mind. People are haunted by a past they don't fully know. They are subjects of violence simply by being embedded in a violent social world. As Rose describes it, people become especially dangerous when they deny their histories and claim false mastery over the future.

24. Desmond and Mpho Tutu believe that reconciliation is the ideal outcome after the granting of forgiveness. But because victims are sometimes so terribly wounded, it is not advisable that they immediately be asked to partner with the people who wounded them. In cases like this, it is better to release the relationship, which means that the victim frees the perpetrator to go away (at least until such time as the victim feels safe and strong enough to be with the perpetrator in a non-damaging manner).

25. Krog, *Conditional Tense,* 200–201.

26. In *No Future without Forgiveness,* Tutu explains that "reconciliation" was not about forgetting or excusing the wrongs done. When the TRC decided to grant amnesty to perpetrators of violence, for instance, they were not allowing perpetrators to go "scot-free." The perpetrators had to apply for amnesty (the Amnesty Committee received over 7,000 applications but granted just over 1,000), and they had to make a public confession about what they did. Confession was not easy, since it brought into public view many horrors that had been done in secret, and it altered how those confessing were perceived in their own communities. Many lost the respect of their families and communities. Moreover, when perpetrators made their public confessions, they also validated the experiences and the stories of victims, many of whom had not been believed by their communities. Had the TRC demanded a formal trial for each perpetrator instead, the courts would have been jammed with many cases that would not have had enough evidence to reach a verdict or to determine proper compensation. The matter of "proper" compensation was also extremely difficult to determine. What form of compensation, and

what amount, is appropriate when considering the death or maiming of a loved one, or when recalling the torture and (ongoing) trauma of victims? Clearly, there are personal and structural/institutional dimensions to these sorts of questions. What struck Tutu was the modesty of the requests that victims made. Some asked for a tombstone, others for help with medical costs, and others for funding to cover education costs for family members. Moreover, the issue of compensation takes on a radically different character if victims are within a vibrant and supportive community and not alone to fend for themselves.

27. Pumla Gobodo-Madikizela, *Dare We Hope? Facing Our Past to Find a New Future* (Cape Town: NB, 2014), 46. In *A Human Being Died That Night,* Gobodo-Madikizela distinguishes two kinds of memory: "If memory is kept alive in order to cultivate old hatreds, it is likely to culminate in vengeance, and in a repetition of violence. But if memory is kept alive in order to transcend hateful emotions, then remembering can be healing" (103).

28. In this regard, consider the insight (drawn from First Nations peoples' experience in Canada) of Allison Hargreaves and David Jefferess: that reconciliation talk is often a means of evasion. "Reconciliation purports to redress historic suffering and injustice, and in so doing provide an end to non-Indigenous guilt and responsibility . . . But what if we understand reconciliation not as a means to secure closure . . . but rather as a place from which to begin the hard work of rethinking relationships and renegotiating responsibilities?" ("Always Beginning: Imagining Reconciliation between Inclusion and Loss," in *The Land We Are: Artists and Writers Unsettle the Politics of Reconciliation,* ed. Gabrielle L'Hirondelle Hill and Sophie McCall [Winnipeg: ARP Books, 2015], 200).

29. Gobodo-Madikizela, *A Human Being Died That Night,* 139.

30. Eve Fairbanks has chronicled the continuing struggles of Black South Africans for justice in *The Inheritors: An Intimate Portrait of South Africa's Racial Reckoning* (New York: Simon and Schuster, 2022).

31. Tutu, *No Future without Forgiveness,* 281. Tutu recognized that the lessons of the TRC are not confined to South Africa. "If we are going to move on and build a new kind of world community there must be a way in which we can deal with a sordid past. The most effective way would be for the perpetrators or their descendants to acknowledge the awfulness of what happened and the descendants of the victims to respond by granting forgiveness, providing something can be done, even symbolically, to compensate for the anguish experienced, whose consequences are still being lived through today. It may be, for instance, that race relations in the United States will not improve significantly until Native Americans and African Americans get the opportunity to tell their stories and reveal the pain that sits in the pit of their

stomachs as a baneful legacy of dispossession and slavery. We saw in the Truth and Reconciliation Commission how the act of telling one's story has a cathartic, healing effect" (278–79).

7
A Hopeful Architecture

1. Vasily Grossman, "The Hell of Treblinka," in *The Road: Stories, Journalism, Essays,* ed. Robert Chandler (New York: New York Review Books, 2010), 162. In the book, published in late 1944, Grossman overestimated the number killed at Treblinka. Historians now put the figure closer to 800,000. Even so, Grossman understood the ruthless efficiency of this "SS death factory." We now know, from a logistics point of view, that the number could readily have exceeded his 3,000,000 estimate, if limits in transportation hadn't prevented the SS from delivering more Jews to the camp (the demands of total war required that transportation networks serve multiple war aims).

2. Vasily Grossman, *Stalingrad,* ed. Robert Chandler and Yury Bit-Yunan (New York: New York Review Books, 2019), 237. Grossman was not alone in his observation. Etty Hillesum, who experienced firsthand the degradations and horrors of camp life in Westerbork and was herself eventually murdered in Auschwitz, remarked on more than one occasion that "the whole of Europe is gradually being turned into one great prison camp" (*An Interrupted Life: The Diaries, 1941–1943, and Letters from Westerbork* [New York: Henry Holt, 1996], 243). For her, the camps meant displacement, ruthless bureaucracy, despair, claustrophobia, squalid living conditions, barbed wire, the constant threats of violence and execution, and endless barracks "where all hell has been let loose" and where people are commanded to sleep "three to a bed on narrow iron bunks, no mattresses for the men, nowhere at all to store anything, children terrified and screaming, the greatest possible wretchedness" (275, 276).

3. Vasily Grossman, *Everything Flows,* trans. Robert and Elizabeth Chandler, with Anna Aslanyan (New York: New York Review Books, 2009), 55. Grossman was still revising this novel while in the hospital and at the time of his death in 1964.

4. Grossman writes that "men were building what no man needed. All of these projects—the White Sea canal, the arctic mines, the railways constructed north of the Arctic Circle, the vast factories hidden in the Siberian taiga, the superpowerful hydroelectric power stations deep in the wilderness—were of no use to anyone. It often seemed that these factories, these canals and artificial seas in the desert were of no use even to the Soviet State, let alone to human beings. Sometimes it seemed that the only purpose of these

vast constructions was to shackle millions of people with the shackles of labor" (ibid., 153).

5. Ibid., 195. Nadezhda Mandelstam, the partner and literary executor of the poet Osip Mandelstam, describes in her memoir, *Hope against Hope* (New York: Modern Library, 1970), how Stalin's regime created a stupefied people lacking the ability to feel any deep animating emotions (like affection, anger, and fear). She writes, "There was an acute sense of being doomed—it was this that gave rise to an indifference so overwhelming as to be almost physical, like a heavy weight pressing down on the shoulders. I also felt that time, as such, had come to an end" (42). This state of stupefaction created people unable to scream in the face of injustices, and unable to maintain the standards and values that could have guided them toward a more desirable future.

6. Grossman, *Everything Flows*, 202–3.

7. In *Demonic Grounds: Black Women and the Cartographies of Struggle* (Minneapolis: University of Minnesota Press, 2006), Katherine McKittrick says, "Geography is not . . . secure and unwavering; we produce space, we produce its meanings, and we work very hard to make geography what it is" (xi). Failing to understand that geographies are made, people also fail to perceive how "geographies of domination" now work around the globe.

8. Achille Mbembe, *Critique of Black Reason*, trans. Laurent Dubois (Durham, NC: Duke University Press, 2017), 161, 162. Mbembe, a Cameroonian philosopher and political theorist, argues that neoliberal thinking and global capitalism are creating a new form of what Frantz Fanon called the "wretched of the earth": "They are those who are turned away, deported, expelled; the clandestine, the 'undocumented'—the intruders and castoffs from humanity that we want to get rid of because we think that, between them and us, there is nothing worth saving, and that they fundamentally pose a threat to our lives, our health, our well-being. The new 'wretched of the earth' are the products of a brutal process of control and selection whose racial foundations we well know" (177).

9. Christopher Alexander, *The Timeless Way of Building* (New York: Oxford University Press, 1979), 62, 25.

10. Amitav Ghosh, *The Nutmeg's Curse: Parables for a Planet in Crisis* (Chicago: University of Chicago Press, 2021), 38. Ghosh quotes Ben Ehrenreich, who makes the point as succinctly as possible: "Only once we imagined the world as dead could we dedicate ourselves to making it so" (39).

11. Simone Weil, in her remarkable essay "Forms of the Implicit Love of God," describes in a particularly insightful way the connection between self-hatred and one's hatred of the world. She writes, "We all are conscious of evil within ourselves; we all have a horror of it and want to get rid of it . . . It is

the ugliness in us. The more we feel it, the more it fills us with horror. The soul rejects it in the same way as we vomit. By a process of transference we pass it on to the things that surround us. These things, however, thus becoming blemished and ugly in our eyes, send us back the evil that we had put in them. They send it back after adding to it. In this exchange the evil in us increases. It seems to us then that the very places where we are living and the things that surround us imprison us in evil, and that it becomes daily worse. This is a terrible anguish" (in *Waiting for God,* trans. Emma Craufurd [New York: Harper and Row, 1973], 189–90).

12. Quoted in Ghosh, *The Nutmeg's Curse*, 55.

13. Alexander, *The Timeless Way of Building,* 148.

14. Ibid., 535.

15. Christopher Alexander, Sara Ishikawa, and Murray Silverstein, with Max Jacobson, Ingrid Fiksdahl-King, and Shlomo Angel, *A Pattern Language: Towns, Buildings, Construction* (New York: Oxford University Press, 1977), xiii.

16. Alan de Botton, *The Architecture of Happiness* (London: Penguin Books, 2006), 13.

17. Agnes Binagwaho, "Beauty That Transcends," in *Justice Is Beauty: MASS Design Group,* ed. Michael Murphy and Alan Ricks (New York: Monacelli Press, 2019), 94.

18. Ibid.

19. Michael Murphy, "Or, And, Is," in *Justice Is Beauty*, ed. Murphy and Ricks, 27.

20. Quoted in "Conversation: Butaro: The Genesis," *Justice Is Beauty*, ed. Murphy and Ricks, 56. For a description of MASS and video footage of several of their design projects (including the hospital in Butaro), see the MASS Design Group website, https://massdesigngroup.org. See also the profile of MASS on CBS's television program "60 Minutes": Lesley Stahl, "The MASS Model of Community Focused Architecture," October 31, 2021, https://www.cbsnews.com/news/model-architecture-serving-society-60-minutes-2021-10-31/.

21. Binagwaho, "Beauty That Transcends," 95.

22. Ibid., 85.

23. Ibid., 95.

8
A Hopeful Economy

1. Adam Smith, *The Theory of Moral Sentiments*, ed. Knud Haakonssen (Cambridge: Cambridge University Press, 2002), 11. *The Theory of Moral Sentiments* was first published in 1759, nearly two decades before he published

The Wealth of Nations in 1776. Smith considered it to be his most important achievement and revised it multiple times. A sixth edition was published in 1790, the year of his death.

2. Ibid., 12.

3. Smith, *The Wealth of Nations;* Corey Robin, "Empathy and the Economy," *New York Review of Books,* December 8, 2022, https://www.nybooks.com/articles/2022/12/08/empathy-the-economy-being-me-being-you-adam-smith/.

4. Robin, "Empathy and the Economy."

5. Lars Spuybroek, *The Sympathy of Things: Ruskin and the Ecology of Design,* 2nd edition (London: Bloomsbury, 2016), 129.

6. Ibid., xvii. Spuybroek is clear that sympathy is not necessarily conscious, personal, or orchestrated to achieve some predetermined end. "I do not think there is a directive force, but I do think forces tend to calibrate and coordinate with each other and therefore to have a single direction as an outcome, not as a resultant but as an agreement. This puts sympathy closer to animism than to vitalism, since it is not the case that life goes through things but that life is shared between things, as an anima not contained in an object but felt by the other during the aesthetic encounter" (217). This means the focus of philosophical endeavor isn't simply *eudaimonia,* well-being, but *euprepeia,* well-becoming. One could make the theological argument that this is precisely the power of the Holy Spirit: that it enables the forms of becoming-with that are reflected in lives of mutual flourishing.

7. H. J. Massingham, *Remembrance: An Autobiography* (London: B. T. Batsford, 1930), 132.

8. Ibid., 134.

9. Ibid., 135.

10. Georg Simmel, "The Metropolis and Mental Life," in *On Individuality and Social Forms: Selected Writings,* ed. Donald N. Levine (Chicago: University of Chicago Press, 1971), 325.

11. Georg Simmel, *The Philosophy of Money* (New York: Routledge, 2011), 498. "Modern man," says Simmel, "is so surrounded by nothing but impersonal objects" that there are "increasingly fewer points at which the subjective soul can interpose its will and feelings . . . Objects and people have become separated from one another" (499).

12. Simmel, "The Metropolis and Mental Life," 326, 330, 329. Seneca's statement is from his *Moral Letters to Lucilius.*

13. Simmel, "The Metropolis and Mental Life," 327–28.

14. Corey Robin, "The Trouble with Money," *New York Review of Books,* December 22, 2022, p. 75. "A monetary economy is not simply an economy in which money is a factor of exchange. It is an economy 'in which changing

views about the future are capable of influencing,' via money, the overall output of the economy" (74). He is quoting John Maynard Keynes.

15. Kathryn Tanner, *Christianity and the New Spirit of Capitalism* (New Haven: Yale University Press, 2019), 80.

16. Ibid., 84, 178.

17. Herman Daly, "A Journey of No Return, Not a Circular Economy," *Steady State Herald,* April 23, 2019, https://steadystate.org/a-journey-of-no-return-not-a-circular-economy/.

18. I am in substantial agreement with many of the aims and principles that guide Kate Raworth's advocacy for a "doughnut economy": replacing GDP as the primary measure of economic progress; recognizing that persons are not isolated, self-interested maximizers who live to dominate nature but are social beings dependent on nature and ecosystem processes; combating the addiction to growth and recognizing that "development" takes many forms; advocating for regenerative designs that acknowledge and build upon feedback loops; and recognizing that economies are embedded in societies and nature. Where I hesitate is in the characterization of natural systems as presenting us with an "ecological ceiling." I believe the image of an economy as a rooted plan does a better job of characterizing natural and social systems as the "soils" that feed us and that we must nurture in return. For more on the doughnut economy see Doughnut Economics Action Lab (DEAL), at https://doughnuteconomics.org; and Raworth's book *Doughnut Economics: Seven Ways to Think Like a 21st-Century Economist* (White River Junction, VT: Chelsea Green, 2017).

19. Aidee Guzman's work is profiled in Liz Carlisle's *Healing Grounds: Climate, Justice, and the Deep Roots of Regenerative Farming* (Washington, DC: Island Press, 2022), 101. Carlisle describes several pioneers in the regenerative agriculture movement who are working to heal injustices done to the land and to the Indigenous peoples and communities of color that have worked with the land for centuries. She concludes that our society's "entire way of relating to the land—and with each other" is what needs to change. "The extraction of carbon from soils was just one integral piece of a much larger process of extraction, a process that included the theft of indigenous lands, the forced enslavement of millions of Africans, and the extortion of immigrant labor. To repair the soil, we need to repair it all" (176).

20. Robin Wall Kimmerer, *Braiding Sweetgrass: Indigenous Wisdom, Scientific Knowledge, and the Teachings of Plants* (Minneapolis: Milkweed Editions, 2013), 183 (italics in the original).

21. For detailed information about the work of The Industrial Commons see its website, https://theindustrialcommons.org/, and the short video presentation "Molly Hemstreet: Crafting a Sustainable Economy in Appalachia,"

https://www.youtube.com/watch?v=qi_Ttx8RqPo, narrated by Molly Hemstreet, the co-executive director.

22. For a description of the major tenets of the social solidarity economy, see the statement of the Intercontinental Network for the Promotion of Social Solidarity Economy (RIPESS), "Global Vision for a Social Solidarity Economy: Convergences and Differences in Concepts, Definitions and Framework," February 2015, at https://www.ripess.org/wp-content/uploads/2017/08/RIPESS_Vision-Global_EN.pdf.

23. My account of the Mondragon Corporation is based on Nick Romeo's essay "How Mondragon Became the World's Largest Co-Op," *New Yorker,* August 27, 2022, https://www.newyorker.com/business/currency/how-mondragon-became-the-worlds-largest-co-op.

24. In *Two Cheers for Politics: Why Democracy Is Flawed, Frightening—and Our Best Hope* (New York: Basic Books, 2022), Jedediah Purdy describes how financial markets often function as an anti-politics because they stifle the forms of democratic participation that enable people to determine the rules by which they will govern themselves and each other. He observes that "every market that has ever been defended as natural and inevitable was built by political will and effort" (218).

Epilogue

1. Erin Manning makes the point succinctly: "It is out of relation that the solitary is crafted, not the other way around: relation is what an object, a subject is made of" (*The Minor Gesture* [Durham, NC: Duke University Press, 2016], 51). Speaking this way does not dissolve ideas of the self, agency, and responsibility. Instead, it makes them communal and ecological. Though people regularly assume an "active voice," exerting their will upon their world, each person lives in the "middle voice," which means having to constantly negotiate a world that intersects, inspires, interrupts, and informs what one is able to do. When "I" think, speak, or move, I always also communicate the thoughts, speech, or movement of others within and through me. This point is of immense significance because it means that to heal and empower people, we must also heal and nurture the communities and places through which they live.

2. Martha Graham, "I Am a Dancer," in *The Routledge Dance Studies Reader,* ed. J. Richard Giersdorf and Y. Wong (London: Routledge, 2019). Retrieved January 12, 2024, from https://search.credoreference.com/articles/Qm9vaoFydGljbGU6NTQoMzI=?aid=100473.

3. Richard Sennett, *Together: The Rituals, Pleasure and Politics of Cooperation* (New York: Penguin Books, 2012), 8. A massive infrastructure con-

sisting of banks, insurance companies, suburbia, grocery stores, and the internet (to name a few elements) has been created to minimize our need of others.

4. Nuar Alsadir, *Animal Joy: A Book of Laughter and Resuscitation* (Minneapolis: Graywolf Press, 2022), 25–26, 9. Alsadir observes that "our preoccupation with perfecting our exteriors, our profiles—which often determine what we have access to in the social world—has caused us to lose touch with our interiors. The dominant issue bringing people into my office for psychoanalysis is the sense that, after sacrificing so much to achieve the lives they had dreamed of, they're unable to experience the pleasure they had expected to accompany those ideal lives they labored to construct" (5).

5. Graham, "I Am a Dancer."

6. I am grateful to Paiter for sharing his insights with me about improvisation and dance.

7. Graham believed practice is central to dance performance and to the performance of a life. It is through dedicated practice that the shape of achievement, the sense of self, and the satisfaction of spirit are achieved. "To practice means to perform, in the face of all obstacles, some act of vision, of faith, of desire. Practice is a means of inviting the perfection desired" ("I Am a Dancer").

Acknowledgments

It is a joy to acknowledge the many people who have inspired, challenged, and encouraged me in the writing of this book. I begin with a team of scholars that participated in a multiyear Henry Luce Foundation–funded project entitled “Facing the Anthropocene.” Over two summer seminars, and then in ongoing conversations, Jedediah Purdy, Janet Soskice, Tim Ingold, Kate Brown, Douglas Kysar, Robin Kimmerer, Robert Macfarlane, Willie Jennings, Kate Rigby, Willis Jenkins, Joyce Chaplin, Alyssa Battistoni, Micah Muscolino, and Radhika Khosla became treasured colleagues and friends as they shared their insights, probing, wisdom, worry, laughter, and good sense. Multiple enduring questions were on the table: What sort of a world are we in? Who is the human (*anthropos*) that has brought about this world and this life-altering context? What is an economy for? How should we reimagine the domains of law and politics in a climate-crisis world? What is the meaning and the point of a human life? I will not ever forget the pleasures of being in such thoughtful and stimulating company. I am deeply grateful to Jonathan VanAntwerpen, Program Director for Religion and Theology at the Henry Luce Foundation, and to the Provost’s Office and staff at the Kenan Institute for Ethics at Duke University for giving the financial and logistical support that made this project possible. I also want to thank the Issachar Fund and its president, Kurt Berends, for providing a sabbatical grant that enabled the uninterrupted time to write this book.

I am grateful for the numerous friends and colleagues who discussed this project with me and, in some instances, read drafts of the chapters: Gretchen Ziegenhals, Greg Jones, Luke Olsen, Jane Bennett, Dipesh Chakrabarty, Jennifer Lawson, Bill McKibben, James C. Scott, Keith Meador, Dan Vermeer, Martin Smith, Don Ruzicka, Peter Storey, Ellen Davis, Luke Mincey, Paiter Van Yperen, and Luke Bretherton. Thanks, too, to Sarah Neff, who compiled the index of this book. I am especially grateful to Wendell Berry for his friendship and for granting me permission to quote several lines from his poem "In Rain." Jennifer Banks, Senior Executive Editor for Religion and the Humanities at Yale University Press, provided early encouragement, gave the best advice on how to conceive and execute the writing of the manuscript, and offered numerous helpful suggestions on the completed version. Mary Pasti did a superb job copyediting the manuscript and brought much-needed clarity to a number of my ideas. The reader reports from anonymous reviewers for the press also offered wise counsel that made this book much better than it would have otherwise been. Whatever errors and shortcomings remain fall to me as one who did not listen well enough.

As I finished writing this book, my family welcomed Lila, our first grandchild, into this world. Her arrival has been a source of more gratitude and joy than I can say. Lila's world, however, and the future she will live into, is, in multiple respects, considerably diminished when compared to the one I entered sixty years ago. My prayer is that this book contributes to the creation of a world that inspires her and her generation's hope, and that it equips all of us to cultivate communities and construct built environments that bear witness to our cherishing of them.

Index